T0147124

Body BLAME

Beat Emotional Eating and Reclaim Your Life

BRYANNA HEARTLEY

Balboa Press books may be ordered through booksellers or by contacting:

Balboa Press
A Division of Hay House
1663 Liberty Drive
Bloomington, IN 47403
www.balboapress.com.au
1 (877) 407-4847

Print information available on the last page.

ISBN: 978-1-5043-0001-8 (sc)
ISBN: 978-1-5043-0002-5 (e)

Balboa Press rev. date: 12/02/2015

While the case studies and references to the experiences described in this book are based on real interactions with real persons, the names, professions, locations, and many other biographical details have been changed to preserve their privacy and anonymity. As well, peoples' experiences have been conflated while others divided, as there were many instances from which to choose a sample that represented a theme. The focus of the book is on my reactions and how they affected my body and thus my life. This is not an autobiography in the strictest sense. There are many details omitted and changed.

In particular, with regards to processing memories in EMDR therapy, not every detail of a memory is given and not every memory that was evoked is included, and some specific details are generalised to protect the identity of others with some substitutions occurring.

Contents

Preface ... xiii
Acknowledgements ... xxiii

Chapter 1 The Body Remembers ... 1
Chapter 2 Weight Obsessed ... 19
Chapter 3 The Genesis of Emotional Eating ... 39
Chapter 4 Breathe, Bree; Breathe! ... 63
Chapter 5 Childhood ... 87
Chapter 6 On the Other Side of Sixteen ... 111
Chapter 7 On the Edge of My Life ... 147
Chapter 8 Repair or Rupture, Realisation, and Recovery ... 175

Bibliography and Suggested Reading ... 201
About the Author ... 207
Endnotes ... 209

To H, my Herald

A friend who will not let you betray yourself is a friend indeed.
—Bill Plotkin, *Soulcraft*

Life is not a private affair. A story and its
lessons are only made useful if shared.
—Dan Millman, Preface, *Way of the Peaceful Warrior*

Preface

GENESIS OF THE BOOK

I came that they may have life, and have it abundantly.
—John 10:10

Two and a half years ago I began a journey to recover my health. Instead of accepting that the state my body was in was an inevitable consequence of being sixty-six years old, I examined various physical symptoms, uncovered their history, and reprocessed the emotional connections. I discovered that once those emotional issues were addressed, the physical manifestations disappeared. I also found that if they reappeared, directing my attention to the underlying emotional causes proved far more useful than visiting my doctor for medication.

On December 9, my spouse of more than forty years, Daniel, sat me down to view a DVD of Joe Cross's documentary *Fat, Sick, and Nearly Dead.* I was shocked at the descriptions of what being fat actually meant health-wise, beyond the distress I felt about being unattractive. I was aware of many health issues. I was booked on the fifteenth for an endoscopy to investigate my reflux that was unresponsive to medication, as well as a colonoscopy. I had experienced asthma that was not responding to normal treatment. I was obese. I realized that if I did not lose weight, I could become very ill indeed. I bought kale, celery, granny smith apples, ginger, and cucumbers the next day and began "the mean, green juice fast."

"Write that book." His hand, fingers pointing, was outstretched toward me. His eyes held mine. I felt quite strange, but I knew what the book was. It was as though it was already in my head and only needed the time for me to write it. The idea of writing such a book had not been there before he spoke.

It was Ash Wednesday. The packed church was alive with banners and music. A huge screen filled the sanctuary. Along with the rest of the congregation, I had queued up the middle aisle so the priest could sign the ashes in a cross on my forehead. Mass was over and outside was dark. I waited expectantly for the lay preacher to begin speaking.

The previous November, in an unprecedented fashion, my parish priest, before he said the final prayers at Mass, asked me by name to a meeting after Mass. "And bring your husband too," he said. On the way to the front of the church, I told Dan that I was puzzled and I didn't know anything about it.

At that meeting of some twenty people, the priest told us about inviting a lay evangelist for a weeklong visit. We agreed to support the parish event, and in the following months, I participated in a minor way in organizing it. Father enthusiastically endorsed it as an inspirational, life-changing event, but he did not want to be the driving force, as it was for spiritual renewal of the parishioners and needed their commitment to work.

Six months later we sat there, the church more colourful than usual, Dan by my side. The evangelist began to share his story. His awareness of his journey with Christ had begun forty years earlier. I realized mine had begun sixty years before, as I was aware of a real and personal relationship with Christ from the age of four.

I listened intently, oblivious of most of my surroundings but aware of Dan. The lay preacher related how several years earlier he had drastically changed his holiday plans because he believed the Lord wanted to tell him something. While visiting St. Peter's Basilica in Rome, he felt compelled to return the next day. He cancelled his family's travel plans for Paris. Unusually, when he returned, St. Peter's Basilica was closed for an important church event. After wandering around outside, he became angry and demanded God let him know what he was supposed to do. He heard he was to lose weight and fix up his relationships with his spouse and family in preparation for the work he was going to be directed to do.

I breathed a sigh of relief. By juicing, I had lost seventeen kilograms (thirty-eight pounds) in the previous two months since watching the Joe Cross DVD. I felt I was on the way, that I had already begun the journey. I was dismissive of the need to work on relationships and did not think that part of his message had anything to do with me. How wrong I was!

He asked, "What would you do if Jesus spoke to you today?"

I held my breath. My focus was totally on his face and voice. Jesus had spoken to me three days earlier. I had woken to hear my name clearly spoken in a mid-tonal male voice. It was Sunday.

The readings at church had asked, "Who shall I send? Who will be my messenger?" In my heart I answered, "Here I am. Send me." We had sung "The Galilee Song," a hymn by Father Frank Anderson, MSC. It had always called to me about leaving my familiar life to follow my heart, but it never seemed appropriate for my life. I had a husband and a family. I felt a profound stirring in my soul, and I was afraid of what might be demanded of me. I was afraid that "down the future of my years" I would have to go "past horizons that I know" (verse 3).

I did not know then what my message was nor to whom I was to give it. I felt I was about to find out.

"What would you do if the Lord spoke to you?" he asked again. "Write that book."

I turned to Dan, who seemed to acknowledge something profound had just happened. I had told him earlier about being called by name on the previous Sunday. I was aware of tightness in my stomach, afraid he might want to discourage me and that I would have to plough through against his unspoken opposition. I was concerned he might not be enjoying it, though afterward he was engaged in looking at the material and purchasing some items and he indicated he wanted to return. We attended each of the meetings held during the following week.

The book actually needed a lot more than writing. It began as a record of my journey, a journey that took me further and deeper than I knew I could go. I imagined the book was about ageing and how to maintain health in the face of a lot of negativity surrounding the ageing populations in the world's advanced economies. I thought it would be about overcoming the negative thinking that saw ageing as deterioration and the reason for the existence of many illnesses, especially obesity. I conceived the book to be part of a defence for my generation as we were blamed for economic woes because of a predicted burden of health needs.

However, I find I am claiming the right of mature women to create a new paradigm for the last quarter of their lives, beyond the roles of wife, mother, and grandmother. I did not realize I needed to live that experience first. In examining the emotions that underlay my need to eat, I discovered anxiety that was ever present throughout my life. I found there were many triggers in my marriage, my profession, and in many relationships that activated anxiety about my lack of worthiness. This had been so subtle I had not always recognized it. It lay out of my awareness and governed my life. The six-year-old girl within me, who had been traumatized, effectively made my life choices.

As it says in the Bible, the truth set me free. Once I understood the emotional life of my soul through dealing with the effects of my emotions on my body, I was free to make decisions about the rest of my life in a manner I had never been free to do before. I had no idea the journey would result in my divorcing the man who had been the centre of my life for forty-seven years or the estrangement from some of my children and their families. I did not know how terribly unhappy I really was beneath the veneer of motherhood and marriage.

My book is not only about teaching others how to live healthily by dealing with their emotions, but it became the vehicle for me to understand how my emotions had driven my life choices at a subconscious level and how they had affected my physical body. The journey has taken me beyond my childhood and its fears, through understanding, and to a place of self-discovery and self-actualization.

It took months for the story to unfold. I was encouraged along the way to continue writing, just as the lay preacher had been encouraged to develop his ministry. He related how little things happened to make his calling to the lay ministry a reality. He never had to seek out the help he needed, because it came as long as he went where he was called, even when it seemed ridiculous. I received further encouragement through his mail-out to participants.

Six months after his mission to my parish, his message concerned Luke 5:1–11, where Simon was asked to go out to fish again, even though he had spent all night fishing and had caught nothing. Miraculously, he then caught so many fish they almost broke the net.

By this time I had separated from Dan.

I found the reflection on this reading incredibly powerful. God takes the opportunity to have us begin something new at the time when we think we have finished. I had important work to do. It was not the time to retire from my profession as a psychologist. I have a great sense of satisfaction when I witness others overcome anxiety, depression, and trauma. However, I was considering retirement because of my age of sixty-five and because I was being urged to do so. Dan wanted to know what I wanted the money for, and my friends thought their retirement was wonderful and couldn't understand why I continued to work.

There is a pattern to my life. I have often found myself going in the opposite direction from everyone else. I feel I have always been swimming upstream. I am doing what I have always done. I find it amazing to find myself here yet again! This journey could be seen as the latest manifestation of my tendency to find myself wondering why I am making choices so differently from my peers. I see my past predilection for going against the tide a confirmation that I am as right in this choice as I was in my earlier ones.

For instance, as young as eleven, I chose to attend the local all-girls high school when classmates chose the more distant and selective all-girls high school. None of them stayed on beyond the third year, leaving school at fifteen, which in 1961 was the norm for Australian girls, when only 10 per cent finished high school.

When I went to university, I continued to go against what 97 per cent of girls did, and I was the first person, male or female, in my family to do so. Furthermore, I majored in mathematics at university to become a teacher at a time when girls weren't supposed to be good at mathematics.

I was always passionate about what I chose to do, investing myself fully, whether it was in teaching, motherhood, cooking, entertaining, church or study. Of the nine pregnant women in the housing estate where I spent the first years of my marriage, I was the only one who breastfed. Only 10 per cent of women even began breastfeeding their babies at that time, but I breastfed my firstborn for more than a year.

Rather than enjoying a quiet year of maternity leave with my last baby, I enrolled in a postgraduate psychology program. At fifty-three, as a member of the student welfare team, I found myself hiking up mountains, caving, and abseiling into a cavern a hundred feet below, despite having never done such things in my life, so some students could have a wilderness experience to challenge them and motivate them to grow.

Rather than joining my peers in retirement at fifty-five, I opened my private psychology practice. At fifty-eight, I began training in

EMDR (eye movement desensitization and reprocessing), a form of psychotherapy, as clients who were referred to me came with increasingly more complicated presentations. (An EMDR therapist helps the client combine eye movements with remembering traumatic material. The therapist guides the process and assists the client to cope with the emotions that are generated, ensuring they are not overwhelmed and have the resources to assist them throughout the therapy.)

The personal work I undertook while learning EMDR was an important foundation for the journey I recorded in this book. Indeed, without EMDR therapy, I am unsure I would have explored the complexity of the interconnecting memories after uncovering the role emotional eating played in my life, although I did use other methods.

With financial security after four decades of marriage, travelling the world, experiencing the possibility of indulging and doing nothing or whatever I wanted, with a marvellous family that perceived me as the mortar that held it all together, and my friends happily settling into preparation for their golden wedding anniversaries, I divorced Dan.

These are but a few instances where I made choices that I still consider the best ones to have made. My choices always put me outside the mainstream of my peer group, and my recent choices are the same. Perhaps like Job, all I have built up during my life will appear to be taken away from me, but I know this is the only way I can be true to my life purpose. I do not understand the full extent of what I am to do, become, or go, but there is a sense of and confidence in my choices as I begin this unexpected chapter in my life.

Writing became something that had to be done. Many little encouragements to continue have occurred. One of the greatest confirmations was when a woman at church, one of many during those months of writing, came up to me after Mass wanting to know what I had done. Something about my face, she said, dismissing with her hands the notion that all she could see was a smaller me. "No," she said. "It's the peacefulness in your face."

At a conference, delivering a workshop on emotional eating, I used a life-sized photo of myself from before I lost weight. The overwhelming response to that photograph has been how depressed I looked. People who have known me for many decades have difficulty recognizing it as me, even if they knew me during that period. They tell me I looked like I did twenty years ago.

I hope sharing my journey gives you a way to find the abundance in your life that is there. I hope to be a light to you, no longer hiding under a bushel.

There have been many changes in my life over these past two years as I have taken responsibility for the choices I have made throughout my life. I note that the blocks I found on my journey forced me to develop into who I am. My anxiety led me to create calmness for my children, students, and clients. Misogyny led me to value the feminine as shown through my years with a mother's support association. Isolation led me to include others. Fear of failure led me to become capable and to encourage it in my children, students, and clients. Lack of money encouraged me to find financial independence. Lack of intimacy led me to learn about communication and to help others communicate. Denigration taught me gratitude to appreciate what others do. Confusion has encouraged me to learn and provide information for others. Lack of empathy has led me to develop empathy for all. Not being listened to encouraged my learning to be an active listener. Insecurity made me create security for my children and clients. These blocks motivated me to follow my life purpose.

The life I seemed to have left is part of my journey, albeit a long part during which I developed the talents I needed. This book was not written to blame anyone or anything other than to understand how my body remembered and how I used this understanding to heal. I accept that I co-created my life and do not blame any of the co-creators.

I had access to professional help and used it. If you try to process things on your own, be aware of your need for safety. Your brain has shied away from these memories for a reason, believing you can't cope. You may be better off seeking professional help than going it alone. Although it has been said that the doctor who treats himself has a fool for a patient, a doctor who does not disinfect and treat a minor cut would be foolish indeed. If treating the cut exceeds your expertise, please seek help.

Acknowledgements

I am extremely grateful to my friend and colleague, whose care was an exemplary example of the best a friend can give. As she shared her story, I was able to share mine. Beginning with concerns about ageing brains, illness, and our own weight gains over the years, she reminded me how wonderful that connection with another woman could be, so I reconnected with others who had waited patiently for me to see them.

Giving me refuge in her home when I needed to leave my marital home and allowing me the space to centre myself, she listened to me relate what I had been writing, wisely leading me to label behaviour that had confused me all my life. She read my book through more than once, offering useful insights and, even after relocating to another city, returning many times to give me support through a difficult, distressing period that occurred when I had thought all would have been resolved.

Relationships with my sister and sister-in-law became closer and more loving than I ever knew possible. I thank them for their patience and hundreds of hours of phone calls. I thank my younger sister especially for hearing my need and travelling to be with me.

Friendships strengthened past the dinner party conversations once more into connectedness. I have been able to be who I am with people I have known all my adult life without presenting a persona that hid me from them and myself. I thank them for their encouragement and preference for the person I am rather than the one I had portrayed for so long. Reuniting with classmates has deepened my understanding of our shared experiences and coloured faded sepia memories.

I acknowledge my family of origin too: my parents, who carried their own burdens and whom I loved; my former husband, Daniel, who has his own story that I did not attempt to retell or interpret as I presented my reactions to what I perceived; my children and their families, who have given me much love during their lifetimes; and my parish priest and fellow parishioners for the willingness to hear about my journey, showing the patience and charity I have needed.

To the many wonderful teachers I met during my journey I send thoughts of gratitude: the infants teachers that encouraged me to read and play; the primary school teachers that nurtured my love of writing, affirmed my leadership qualities, encouraging my parents to view me as an intelligent child that should be channelled into the academic subjects of languages and mathematics rather than the traditional subjects for girls; the high school teachers that affirmed my achievements and contacted my parents so I could complete high school and then apply for university; my home room teacher for noticing how genuinely I prayed when repeating The Lord's Prayer at the beginning of every school day; the university teachers against whose opinions I found my strength; my supervisors in the education departments who mentored me and the many specialist trainers that have shared so much.

I am grateful for the many affirmations I have received from the universe, sometimes from strangers at shops, banks, hairdressing and beauty salons, or in doctors' surgeries. I appreciate the acceptance and applause from colleagues as I have publicly and privately shared my insights and journey.

During my studies, a fellow postgraduate student believed, because I was Catholic, I would not be able to assist a pregnant teenager should she choose to terminate her pregnancy. This shocked me. To help others to make their choices for their lives according to their beliefs has always guided my actions. I realise this is not the case for everyone. I thank my fellow student for raising this ethical question so I could delineate my private beliefs from professional ethics.

Following twelve months of crises, in July 1992, I sat in prayerful meditation questioning what I ought to be doing, with whom and how. I found the answers in my Bible as I opened it three times for guidance. I am grateful my local Presbyterian Church minister taught me to use the Bible for guidance.

Make love your aim, and earnestly desire the spiritual gifts, especially that you may prophesy....he who prophesises speaks to men for their upbuilding and encouragement and consolation.
—1 Cor.14: 1-3

Conduct yourselves wisely towards outsiders, making the most of the time.
—Col. 4:5

Take him, look after him well and do him no harm, but deal with him as he tells you.
—Jer. 39:12

Printed in the front of my annual diaries and framed on the wall of my office, they have served as my mission statement ever since, though I changed the gender! They reflect very well the principles underlying professional codes of ethics of nonmaleficence and beneficence.

My interpretations of the synchronicities that have guided my journey while writing this book may not resonate for everyone. We see through the eyes of our beliefs but they ought not act as barriers to understanding the beliefs of others and respecting their traditions and values. I thank those who shared their life journeys with me whether Orthodox, Coptic, Protestant, Catholic, Salvation Army, Society of Friends, Seventh Day Adventist, Islam, Buddhism, Wicca, agnostic or atheist, and Hindu, or other. I thank clients from the LBGTIQ and indigenous communities for their trust.

To all my wonderful clients from all religions, races, creeds, and cultures for their trust and willingness to seek help, allowing a small pebble to be placed in the ravine so they could begin to build the bridge across to a healthier life, I send my heartfelt gratitude. Transpersonal psychology recognizes that we are spiritual beings having a physical experience, comprising mind, body, and soul. I prefer not to limit spirituality to a creed.

To editor David S. at Balboa, I am indebted for his recognition of the essence of my story as an inspirational memoir and his careful guidance at clarifying that vision as he took me through the process of deleting waffling third-person pseudo-academic commentary.

My most profound gratitude goes to my partner, whose spirituality and empathy is so affirming of my right to be. He shows me that sharing goals, dreams, interests, tasks, and life can be achieved without one human being controlling and manipulating another. He shares his innermost self, showing me that gender isn't a determinate of trust. His willingness to share my journey after I had opened my eyes to where it had taken me is a blessing I never expected.

Chapter 1

THE BODY REMEMBERS

Children are so forgiving. You can treat them like absolute crap, and they still give you a cuddle. Terrible things happen to them, and they never remember them. They are too young to remember. These represented the received wisdom of previous generations when advising young parents in the 1970s. The first inkling I had that little children remember what happens at a physical level, even if they can't tell you what actually occurred was when my eldest son was ten. The children were piling into the blue Sigma to go to the garbage dump with Dan. However, things were not quite organized, and gradually the kids left the car. When there were no other children going, my eldest son decided not to go too, yet I knew he really wanted to. (Some "boy thing," I believe, since I had no idea what the attraction was.)

I puzzled over this, and it occurred to me that the last time he had gone anywhere alone in the car with his dad was when he was two and a half years old. We were visiting my in-laws, and after dinner he suddenly started screaming. Nothing could calm him, and he was obviously in pain.

I was breastfeeding his younger sibling, so Daniel took him to the local hospital, staying until he fell asleep around midnight. He had a strangulating inguinal hernia, and if it had continued he would have needed an operation immediately, but it resolved somewhat. Despite intending to be there before he woke, we weren't, though my mother arrived before us to find him standing at the end of the cot, holding onto the rails, crying. He wanted to go to the toilet, and the nurses didn't seem to understand. The following week he was admitted again and had the operation. Afterward, he clung to my leg for the next six months.

Not knowing if this event was connected to his changing his mind about going to the tip, I told him the story and suggested that if he felt uncomfortable in his tummy when he was alone in the car with his dad, maybe his body remembered even if he didn't. In any case, he didn't continue having the problem, so I thought I was a bit of a genius.

There is much research now supporting this. We know adverse childhood experiences impact people throughout their lives.[i] Children might not have an episodic memory of a particular traumatic event, but their bodies remember.

A few years later, as a school counsellor, I did not have that intimate knowledge of a child's life, yet it was obvious those who were referred to me were highly reactive from past experiences.

I had them imagine the early warning system in the brain, the amygdala, as "Sgt. Amy G. Dala" on guard duty, challenging each bit of information coming in to decide if it is possibly dangerous. If "Sgt. Amy" decides there is danger, she sends out the "troops." Cortisol,

> Physical signs of fight or flight response
>
> The pupils of the eyes dilate to give better peripheral vision so you can see anything sneaking up on you. The hearing becomes more acute to allow you to hear anything approaching. Breathing becomes shallow. The heart pumps blood faster to provide more energy to the limbs. The parasympathetic nervous system is turned off so that the mouth becomes dry, and the digestive tract stops digesting food to save energy. So you experience butterflies in the tummy and may need to urinate and defecate. Hands may become sweaty, and the hair on the back of the neck may rise.

adrenaline, and other stress hormones are released and prepare the body to fight, flee, or freeze.

The body reacts before the brain thinks. When we lived in the wild, it was important for survival to develop this early warning system. If "Sgt. Amy" recognised there was a threat, she would get you ready to grab your spear to kill or to run away from danger. If you could not run or fight, the reaction is to freeze, like a possum being caught by predators. In the latter situation the possum is not playing dead but is actually immobilised and incapable of voluntary movement. When the danger passes, the possum's body trembles, mobilising its muscles so it can run off to safety.

When I noticed a reaction in my body, I could take control. I breathed slowly and gently, relaxed, took control of my body and thoughts, and calmed down. For instance, visiting hospitals caused me to be on alert. Knowing that I'd been left in a hospital when a first grader did not remove the distress. I did, however, know how to breathe and relax. To desensitize, I relaxed, visualized a hospital scene, and practised staying relaxed while imagining the scene. In this way I did not become phobic about being in a hospital. My level of distress did not become debilitating. I could take my children to hospital if required, but I always needed to calm myself.

I taught children how to desensitize from the things that caused them to react. Students who had a school phobia would begin the day with me as I guided them through relaxation exercises. Children who were irritable with siblings or argumentative with peers benefited from the exercises. In a questionnaire after they had completed ten sessions—many admitting they had signed up to avoid mathematics or some other disliked class—they reported positive effects on their relationships and improvements in their ability to concentrate. In this way, at one high school I taught 44 per cent of the student body how to desensitize on disturbing triggers. This was very good for my self-esteem, and I felt very useful, capable, and confident.

Individual teachers who asked me to conduct a relaxation class with their students would also participate in the relaxation exercises, and then they sometimes asked for additional help in targeting a particular personal problem. This contributed to my interest in seeing adults when I opened my private practice as a psychologist after retiring from my position with the department of education.

Using relaxation and visualisation of disturbing events to desensitize is very time-consuming with adults as they have so many triggers from past experiences and have to do a lot of homework themselves, which I supported by taping the training sessions for them. Imagine "Sgt. Amy" taking a photo each time she sends out the troops and keeping that photo album handy, as she needs to recognise anything that has already proved dangerous. I found the older the adult, the thicker the photo albums. Each "photo" contained what was heard, seen, smelled, felt in the body, tasted, touched, and thought. Everything is locked in the nervous system. I looked for other methods, and this was how I became interested in EMDR (eye movement desensitization and reprocessing) therapy.[1]

In 1987, Dr. Francine Shapiro began examining the phenomenon whereby remembering traumatic material was combined with eye movements to reduce the intensity of disturbing thoughts. The innate natural healing for the mind occurs during REM (rapid eye movement) sleep. This is disrupted when events overwhelm the system. It is replicated in EMDR therapy. Marco Pagani (2013, Journal of EMDR Practice and Research, 7(1), 29) noted that EMDR

---

[1] With more than twenty years of research supporting this therapy, EMDR (eye movement desensitization and reprocessing) has gained approval from a wide range of organizations, including the World Heath Organization, the Australian Psychological Society, and the Clinical Division of the American Psychological Association as providing the best evidenced-based therapy available for PTSD, and it has been adapted for many other psychological issues. Other modalities such as auditory and kinaesthetic can be utilised effectively too. Discussion of the actual mechanism by which the brain reprocesses the information and desensitizes includes noting that by having a client pay attention to the traumatic material and pay attention to eye movements (called dual attention), working memory is affected in a beneficial manner. For further information, visit http://emdraa.org.

was "the first psychotherapy with a proven neurobiological effect" as shown with EEG (electroencephalography) during therapy sessions.

As I tell my clients, we can use EMDR therapy to move the photographs that "Sgt. Amy" has in her photo albums to another album for old, faded photos that are not connected with the upsetting feelings. Sometimes we are able to process a whole section in one session so there is no homework. EMDR therapy integrates many elements of other psychotherapies and has a positive effect on the way the brain processes information.

I had heard about EMDR therapy in the 1990s but it was considered by my immediate superiors to be too unorthodox for use in schools. As well, there was little time available for therapy, per se. However, when EMDR therapy was advertised in the APS (Australian Psychological Society) journal, I decided it must have become more established, and I was eager to learn more about it. I undertook the basic training in 2006. Two years later I attended some advanced training in a residential setting. I did not realise at the time that this would be a significant beginning for the rest of my life journey.

My Experience with EMDR Therapy

At the training, in order to practise what we had learned, all the clinicians divided into pairs, with each of us taking a turn as a client and as a therapist. We were asked to focus on an actual issue that held some emotional charge. By this I mean that when a person thinks about an event, there is some degree of discomfort.

We were instructed to choose something from our childhood that had a level of disturbance of around SUDS = 5. That is about half way. SUDS is an acronym for Subjective Units of Distress Scale. It is a self-rating score for distress from a neutral or calm of zero to the most distressed of 10 out of 10.

I searched my childhood memories and no disturbing memory came to mind. I believed I had desensitized all distressing events through my studies, other courses, and even in earlier EMDR training. I did not realize then that I was emotionally overeating and that this operated in a way to block access to my being consciously aware of some emotional distress. I later discovered there were many possibilities.

The course leader suggested as an alternative I choose something mildly irritating or disturbing in the present. It must have been the idea of something being irritating that triggered the thought. I would feel annoyed if when I went to brush my teeth, Dan used the toilet. Perhaps it was true that as we had been married so long it should not bother me. Yet it did. I interpreted my reactions as indicating there was something wrong with me for not being tolerant.

Following the other trainee's instructions during the training session, I closed my eyes, focusing on my body. I became aware of my teeth clenching, my face contorting with disgust, my lips puckering, my eyes screwing up, my throat constricting. I was asked when I had felt those body sensations before in my life. I was asked what emotions did I feel in connection with those body sensations. The emotions acted as a bridge, taking me from the present to the past. Travelling back through the years, holding those feelings in focus, the images that came to me around that disgust were from when I was seven years old.

It was dark; a light shined through the open door. My mother was bending toward me. I saw my mother's face screwed up in disgust and shame. Her skin was smooth, as it remained throughout her life, her brown hair in a long bob, just above her shoulders. At just over five foot, she was plump, and barely thirty. Her green eyes weren't visible in the dim light. She was wearing a dressing gown over her nightgown.

I was on a camp bed, in front of my wardrobe doors. My paternal grandmother was to the left, in my bed under the window, my sister asleep in the other bed. I had defecated in my bed. My mother was exclaiming to my nana, "She has never done anything like this before." I could see the outline of my nana in bed, propped up and leaning forward. Dead at sixty-three, less than a year later, she was very thin and her face wrinkled with ill health and fatigue. Her grey hair was cut severely around her face.

Being with another psychologist, she was able to use EMDR therapy with me on this memory. The SUDS level was way above the halfway target of five, but it was a powerful session. Of course my stated purpose was to be accepting of the normal bowel habits of my spouse of forty years, which did occur, but the most staggering effect was on my own body.

To understand this, we need a little of my personal history around this part of my body. One memory is my mother and her friend giving each of their two daughters enemas. The four of us were lined up in the bathroom. I have no idea the reason for this, but it was gross and embarrassing taking turns releasing the contents into the empty bathtub.

When I was eighteen, I visited the family doctor for the problem of bleeding from the anus. Aside from the shame and humiliation of seeking advice, there was total embarrassment when, during the examination, his hair seemed to brush my bottom. This all came up during EMDR therapy desensitization and was processed. I had haemorrhoids, and I was advised about diet.

From then on it became important for me to eat plenty of fibre and drink water to keep me regular. Porridge with the addition of several spoonfuls of bran was the usual breakfast for most of my life. Away from home I would sometimes experience quite severe problems with constipation. I always feared being away from home lest I couldn't follow a proper diet. This made me very anxious, and to deal with the anxiety I would often take my own breakfast, despite the fact that it did not seem to work.

I also felt ashamed, so I never talked about it. When I visited my doctor to discuss pain in my side and was diagnosed with irritable bowel syndrome (IBS), I never mentioned that there was a specific problem of constipation occurring only when I was not at home.

My preoccupation was hidden and became hidden from myself in many ways.

Prunes by the pound were always on stand-by. On one of our first overseas holidays in Asia, I woke one morning unable to do up my jeans. Worn the day before, the zipper was now a hand-width apart! I had not emptied my bowels for ten days. This was despite consuming banquets of Asian food at every meal. *Buy me some prunes, now!* was my plea. I could not mention how much discomfort I was suffering until it became unbearable.

This was a pattern in my life. Away from home, I would become constipated. This fear made me quite anxious about going away for any length of time. I did not talk about it. No one else had any difficulty. I accepted that it was my weird problem and peculiar deficit.

I worried silently, hoping that if I ate enough vegetables and drank enough water I would be all right, but I rarely was. Even a weekend away, or sleeping over at friends' houses after a late night were problems that interfered with regularity. Longer overseas holidays were problematic.

Haemorrhoids, bleeding from the anus, concerns about how old I was, and the medical history of my family that included people dying from cancer found me needing to have colonoscopies as well. I accepted this was the way my system worked, as if I had a uniquely different body from others.

Returning to the story of the 2008 EMDR training, I had not emptied my bowels since arriving four days earlier at a beautiful resort in the country, although as usual I had made no comment about it. In the evening, after processing the event from when I was seven, which included associated memories of the other times I have mentioned, I was able to use the toilet easily without effort. I have had no further problems with constipation ever since.

I do not need any particular foods or worry about not having it. I have travelled throughout Europe for three months and been regular.

Processing being irritated by Daniel using the toilet when I cleaned my teeth began to unlock the memories of my body. I thought his regularity annoyed me but I was so little in touch with my feelings at this point that I could only allow myself to experience irritation instead of recognising that my feelings were far more complicated.

So what?

I would often say I was like an old car that needed to take extra time for service to keep running. I began to expect things to go wrong and be more difficult within my body, because I was older, without actually recognising the history of that part of my body's experience. My doctors never suggested there might be some emotional component to a physical problem. Rather, I believed I should expect things to deteriorate. However, repeatedly, with clients I was finding that a physical problem was often ameliorated and even eliminated through processing memories using EMDR therapy.

> Ben's story
>
> Ben, fifty-five, had general anxiety about his health. Attending a doctor's appointment was problematic for him, and he would postpone for months before making one, despite catastrophizing about the symptom (in other words, assuming he would die). A recurring symptom was a painful tension in his lower gut. We eventually identified that he was circumcised as a preschooler. Processing and desensitization were quickly completed. Several years later he was able to report that he no longer obsessed about medical tests or annual checkups but took them in his stride.

In *Thinking, Fast and Slow* (Kahneman 2013, 53), Kahneman refers to an experiment where young undergraduates were influenced to walk more slowly down a hall after they worked on a word puzzle that contained words associated with old age. I wondered how much more we who identify ourselves as being old are influenced to act at being old.

The belief that if we have a pain it means something is wrong is embedded in our psyche. After all, if I put my hand into a fire, it will hurt, and I will pull it out quickly. It is a basic protective instinct, but recognising that pain and discomfort can also be part of a memory is not instinctual. In fact, people don't want to believe that, because then they may have to believe it is all in their heads—they are crazy, have a mental illness, are a hypochondriac, or have psychosomatic illnesses or some somatic disorder. It is much safer to go with the prevailing cultural mindset. "Of course you have more aches and pains because you're old."

EMDR Therapy on my Own

In 1997, I went on my first holiday to Europe. For the first five days visiting Italy, a lifetime's dream, I had the most excruciating pain in both ears that began as the plane descended.

I accepted that as I had become older, this part of my body was in some way understandably defective as there had been no problem in 1969 when I flew to Esperance for my honeymoon.

I discovered chewing alleviated my inability to tolerate the change in air pressure that I assumed created the pain. Not willing to curtail my travels, preparation for subsequent trips always entailed copious packets of chewing gum, which I would consume for hours. Great wads of gum seemed utterly necessary to stave off any hint of a change in air pressure in the plane, lest my ears reverberate within my head, painfully dominating my mind.

However, some months after the advanced training, I found myself on the way to London chewing gum–free. Not allowed to carry even water on board following 9/11, I was near panic as I sat in my seat, buckled up, the whine of the engines heralding imminent pressure changes and a pain-filled week ahead.

No one else seemed to be panicking. They were chatting and settling into their seats, pulling out books, perusing the in-flight magazines, stowing gear at the last minute. I thought, *Surely other people experience some discomfort? Why don't the flight attendants hand out some sort of remedy? Is it possible, of all these hundreds of people on board, I am the only person about to suffer this way?*

"Ahhh," I said to myself. "Maybe the pain is related to an earlier experience?" Well that wasn't a hard question. It certainly had an easy answer. My childhood was replete with bilateral ear infections, with warmed olive oil inserted and small pads of cotton wool stuffed in the ear canals. There were memories of waking at night, whimpering softly until my mother would come to me. I remember her patting my head until I fell asleep.

I had the kernel of the problem, but there was no other clinician there to assist me with EMDR therapy. However, after all, Dr. Francine Shapiro had discovered the benefit of moving her eyes back and forth across the horizon while she was walking in the park when she was worried, noticing the decrease in her level of distress. Surely I could manage this on my own. Would the back of a chair on a plane suffice for a horizon? It did. After a while I used a horizontal figure eight, or more delightfully followed the sign for eternity for my eye movements, and basically set it up as if I was a therapist with myself as the client.

The image for my target memory was sensing myself lying in bed, the pillow beneath my head, blankets covering me, my ears in pain, in the dark, whimpering, looking at the doorway, waiting for the light to be turned on. I wanted my mother to come in but was afraid to call out lest I woke my sister or father.

My belief about myself was "I can't handle it." In EMDR therapy this is called the negative cognition. We psychologists like special phrases like that.

My preferred positive belief was "I can handle it." This is called the positive cognition.

The extent I believed the positive cognition, known as the validity of cognition (VoC), was five on a scale of one to seven. If it were completely false I would have stated it rated one out of seven. If it were completely true, I would have stated it was seven out of seven. Rating it five out of seven indicates I felt it was more true than false.

I was afraid and felt lonely. I experienced those feelings in my chest.

I rated my SUDS (subjective units of distress scale) at six on a scale of zero to ten, where zero was calm or neutral and ten was as distressing as could be.

I held the image in my mind of lying in bed in the dark, my ears in pain, whimpering, waiting for the light to be turned on, and let my eyes trace a line backward and forward across the back of the chair in front of me. I kept my head still and had removed my glasses, so only my eyes moved. I did not have any way to count the number of times but let myself stop when it felt like it was time. A therapist would have had me do eye movements around twenty-four times or would have watched for subtle signals to tell me when to stop.

I took a slow gentle breath and asked myself what I noticed. Gradually, what I noticed changed. Different thoughts, different emotions, even different memories about myself came up. Each time I kept what came up in my mind and went with it, changing to an eternity symbol for my eyes to trace, as it seemed easier in the confined space of the plane seats. It is normal after a set of eye movements for other thoughts, images, feelings, and body sensations to occur. The goal is that the memory will be processed and the emotions will no longer be evoked by the memory.

I was concerned that it might not work and was dreading in anticipation a pain-filled five days. I was self-conscious in case anyone noticed my eyes zipping back and forth like some madwoman.

Eventually all the tension was gone; I wasn't upset by the memory, but the picture had changed. My mother had come to my bedside, and I had fallen asleep again. My SUDS was zero, and I could now say, "I can handle it." To make sure I could truly handle it, I held in my mind the new image of my mother beside my bed and the thought that *I can handle it*, and I allowed my eyes to go back and forth. I did this several times until I was sure there was no residual tension left in my body.

The plane took off while I was doing this. When it landed and took off again in Singapore, to land at Heathrow twenty-three hours after leaving Australia, I experienced no pain at all on any of the occasions. I haven't since. I don't need to chew. I don't need to drink and swallow. I am okay.

I had frequent earaches as a child. The medical advice concerning my ears and their propensity to develop an abscess had an impact on me in many ways. In discussing this with people of my own age, I find others were given the same advice: do not put your head under water! I took from that advice that there was something inherently defective about my ears and thus me. This affected my enjoyment of the great Australian experience of swimming, surf, and sun. Being a very, very good girl, I did what I was told. I never put my head under water, so I only ever did breast stroke with my head held up high. I never jumped into a pool and certainly never learned to dive.

As a teenager, I was dunked in the surf, but for some reason this was acceptable. I believe it was because it was saltwater, which I was told was good for me. When washing my hair in the bath, I always lay down to dunk my head under the water. I did not notice these exceptions to the rule, but they call into question the medical advice I was given.

It was as if the doctor made an assumption that if I had been swimming, that must be associated with or causing the infection. I think this is a basic error. Correlation is not causation. In fact, it is a very primitive interpretation and the basis of superstitions, that if events occur sequentially, the first caused the second. Children may be excused for believing they caused someone's death by being angry with the person, or their parents' divorce because of their bad behaviour, but it is distressing to realise our medical professionals sometimes revert to this type of primitive thinking.

A few years later I indulged my inner child in the pool. When I kept an eye on my neighbour's children while she looked after her ill mother, I sometimes invited them to take a swim in my pool. I noticed how easily her boys could do handstands and one day decided to try. I was a little woeful in my first few attempts. One of them asked if I would mind being given some tips and took on being my personal trainer. Very quickly I learned to do handstands and tumbles backward and forward.

I congratulated him on winning some firsts in the school swimming carnival. I quickly regretted my enthusiasm when he told me the next year he would be required to dive in and wanted me to teach him. Being competent with theory, I was able to coach him on how to dive. I was afraid he might decide I'd need to learn that skill too but as the swimming season was ending, hopefully there would not be enough time to consider teaching me what had been learned.

The next visit proved to be a sunny, warm day, and there was the sudden realisation that I needed to learn to dive too. Having never jumped into a pool, I undertook that task, and before the hour was out, had managed to dive in and swim freestyle down the pool.

It is really never too late to learn!

Nor is it too late to recognise connections. My ear abscesses never burst nor did I take any medication for them. One night I noticed a pain in my ear connected with feeling lonely and realise that one way I may have acquired the attention I craved from an absent mother was to be in pain. My mother was a rare creature for her era. She returned to paid employment when I was nine or ten. This was not in a profession but in a factory, so it meant she was absent from 6:30 a.m. to 6:00 p.m. every day.

Imagining her patting my forehead actually put me to sleep one night after I had separated from Daniel. It is amazing that I had never lived on my own until the age of sixty-six. I thought it might be an unfamiliar feeling of aloneness, but the realisation that I could and did imagine a gentle caress on my forehead alerted me to the fact that I often felt alone in my childhood. In this journey, I reprocessed many memories and eventually understood how they shaped me.

Some problems frequently appear to worsen with age. The process is that every time we are a little anxious, it is as if we layer each experience on top of every other similar one, and the anxiety increases. This too is a learned behaviour. It is not because we have grown older. It is because we have practised it more.

> Amanda's Story
>
> Her son was graduating in England, but she was so afraid of flying that she could not even bear to book a ticket. Beginning with thinking about flying, phoning to book a ticket, packing, driving out to the airport, and waiting at the airport in a queue to check in, we identified each step.
>
> I taped a session where I taught her how to relax. Once relaxed, I asked her to imagine where she would be when she was thinking about flying to England. She visualised she was in her lounge room. She pictured the floor, the ceiling, the walls, the doors, the windows, the lounge chairs, the cushions, and any other furnishings as vividly as she could. Then she invited into the scene anyone else that would be there, so she imagined her husband and dog, picturing their eyes, faces, clothes, and voices.
>
> Then she thought about travelling to England. She clenched her jaw and tensed her shoulders and her toes curled up. Even though she was not in her lounge room, she experienced the tension. She had unintentionally learned to increase the tension just by practising it when she was thinking about it. As she had learned to tense her body in response to thinking, she could also learn to put the relaxation response in its place. The imaginal exposure was repeated twice. On the third visualisation, her tension lessened.
>
> She proceeded to the next step of ringing up the airline to book a ticket when she remained relaxed about the first step. It was not until she was imagining sitting in her seat inside the aeroplane and hearing the engines whine that she realised the noise was like a dentist drill (which she didn't like).
>
> It took many weeks to process all these steps, but a postcard from her husband thanking me was great acknowledgment of success.

We may take some years to develop the learned behaviour of fear of flying, or open spaces, or leaving the house. It would happen faster if we practised it enough to learn it more quickly! At first you feel a little worried and may even ignore the bodily sensations. Every time you experience those sensations, it is as though you save them up. Each time the event happens, your response becomes stronger. It really is no different from when you learned the times tables or how to spell dinosaur, a word my eldest found daunting when he was nine years old. The more you practise something, the stronger the neural connections become. Despite my successful insight with my son, I gave little thought to the idea that any of my physical complaints had any history other than "this is just my body; I have always been like this." My mother stated that I was healthy until I went to school. I believed I was a sickly child and this accounted for why I developed asthma, sore throats, constipation, irritable bowel, earache, and reflux. Unconsciously I had formed the belief that my body was not as healthy as others'.

I was surprised that each physical problem had an emotional history that accompanied the occurrences of the signs of illness. I found that dealing with the emotions was effective in clearing away the symptoms. Beyond that, I discovered, like my ten-year-old son, that when I had a better understanding of what my body was telling me, I was able to make different decisions. Like him, I was free to do what I wanted and was not governed by unconscious, fear-driven instincts. However, I had a very thick photo album. It was going to take a few years to tackle.

Working It Through

Choose a problem, whether it is seeing someone you don't like, going somewhere you want to bypass, or writing a report or making a phone call you'd rather avoid. To desensitize on it, identify up to twenty small steps involved in the activity that causes you stress.

One way to relax is by becoming mindful of your breathing. Close your eyes. Put your right hand on your solar plexus and your left hand on your chest. Compare your hands to see which moves first and which moves further. In normal natural breathing, the solar plexus (just above your navel and below your breastbone) moves gently. The hand on your chest remains still.

Breathe in through your nose and out through your nose. Count slowly: one, two, three, four. Slow down your breathing. Imagine you are gently inflating a balloon in your tummy as you breathe in and deflating it as you breathe out.

Take a little longer as you breathe out and pause slightly at the end of each breath. Do not force this or hold on. If your mind is distracted, notice the thought, and bring your attention back to you hands, back to your breathing. Let any thoughts turn into clouds and drift away. Sometimes natural abdominal breathing is sufficient to bring about the relaxation response. If not, use the following instructions for progressive muscle relaxation.

Write down a phrase you choose to condition your body to obey. Something like "be calm," "let go," "relax," "let it all go." Begin the progressive muscle relaxation with clenching your hands, one at a time, into a fist. Hold for seven seconds and then relax, saying the phrase you have chosen as you relax the tension. Compare your hand before and after tightening it into a fist, noting if it is more relaxed after tensing it. If it is more relaxed, then you have been carrying tension in your hand. Repeat. Then work through each of the biceps. Repeat. Next focus on your head. Begin with lifting the eyebrows and wrinkling the forehead. Frown, bringing your eyebrows together, scrunch up your eyes, tighten the lips, pucker the mouth, press the tongue against the roof of your mouth, tighten the jaw. Repeat. Roll the head, shrug the shoulders, breathe into the chest, the stomach; arch the back while tightening the small of the back; tighten the muscles in the buttocks, thighs, shins and calves by flexing your feet. Repeat.

Once relaxed, visualise the problem by first picturing the surroundings, then by inviting anyone else into the scene, and then let the event happen. Now scan your body from the top of your head to the bottom of your feet, particularly noting any increase in tension, and tighten those parts of your body and release them. Repeat twice. On the third time, most people experience less tension.

Another way to relax is using a self-hypnosis technique.

Choose a part of your body, like your left arm if you are right handed, or vice versa, to imagine it will grow heavy. Imagine you can see the numerals on a large movie screen as you slowly count back from 10 to 0. Imagine you are going down a series of escalators in a tall building. After each number, tell yourself that your arm is growing heavy, heavier, gradually imagining that you are increasing the weight and inability to move. When you reach zero, you will find that your arm is too heavy to move.

You can practise this before going to sleep and allow yourself to drift off to sleep, or after a few minutes tell yourself to count to three and sit up feeling relaxed and refreshed.

Reflect on what happened. You know your arm has not really changed in size, yet you could programme your mind to believe it had.

Chapter 2
WEIGHT OBSESSED

I couldn't see my toes. I was obese.[2] It was early 2012. I have no idea what my waist measurement was, but it was much greater than the recommended limit of 31.5 inches (80 centimetres).

How did I get here? More importantly, what was I going to do about it? There was so much advice around about how to eat properly, but the more I knew, the worse I ate! What happened? I was out of tune with my own needs.

In 2012, two-thirds of adults in Australia were found to be overweight or obese. The trend is continuing, with 75 per cent predicted to be overweight or obese by 2020.[3] The prediction that I only had a one in four chance of maintaining a healthy weight was very distressing. As I became older, I grew fatter. A pound extra this year and the next, and voilà, I'm fat.

---

2 I was 198 pounds at five foot, five inches. A healthy weight for me was between 110 and 149 pounds. My BMI (body mass index) was 33. It should have been less than 25. (Anything greater than 30 is a marker for obesity.) In metric, this was 90 kilograms when I needed to be between 50 and 68 kilograms.

3 See http://www.modi.monash.edu.au/obesity-facts-figures/obesity-in-australia/ for statistics stating it will be 80 per cent by 2025 if the trend continues.

I felt indignant about what seemed my fate. It is not the fact that I have had another birthday that has caused me to put on a few extra pounds, except perhaps the birthday cake itself may have contributed, along with the brie, the glasses of champagne, and the extra slices of cheesecake consumed at all the other birthdays of all my extensive family and friends during the year. As well, holidays and other celebrations add their weight!

Special occasions when I had a supply of lollies in the lolly jar, as for Christmas and Easter, were dangerous! For Christmas, I loved buying chocolate-coated almonds. The thought of them makes my mouth water. The red, sugar-coated peanuts (known as Boston Baked Beans) and the chocolate ones completed the required set. Once purchased, the jars sat in a row high up in the cupboard, promising delight. I made rules around when I was permitted to open them. Without children in the house, and with the money to replace them, it became easier to open them weeks before Christmas. The restraints of children who would want to share them before the right occasion and the inability to afford replacing them had acted as barriers to indulging in them earlier in my marriage. They sat on the shelf in their tempting plastic bottles reminiscent of the shiny glass bottles my mother used when I was young.

When I realised it was easier to resist buying them early or at all—once in the house, they acted like a magnet, attracting me until I finally succumbed—it became easier to resist the thought of them just under my consciousness, ready to pop up with temptation. Once opened, it took a few days of going past the hiding place in the top of the wardrobe in the spare bedroom, unseen by others, to empty the jar, one surreptitious handful at a time.

This of course leads to chocolate. Who wants to give up chocolate? I admit there has been more than one Easter egg hunt that had to be re-supplied because many of the chocolate eggs mysteriously disappeared prior to Easter Sunday. Again, attempts to hide them from myself would fail.

I chose small chocolate eggs, as large ones were less accessible. It was easier to consume a handful of tiny eggs than it was to break open a large one. I justified this by asserting that the grandchildren received so much candy, I should not add to the amount of chocolate they would consume.

I spent days preparing the Easter egg hunt for the grandchildren. At first it was easy, with only a few grandchildren, but as more babies appeared it became more complicated. With so many tiny eggs to hide, a few dozen going missing was not obvious to anyone, even myself.

There were also special chocolate eggs bought for the table for Easter Sunday lunch. Baskets of eggs were placed around the house. Special bowls were purchased. Dan would comment that I spoiled the children by buying so many eggs, but perhaps I had to buy more to make amends for having eaten them earlier. Worse still, it allowed me to consume as many as I wanted without it being obvious, even to myself. I could avoid being shamed if no one knew—except I felt the shame anyway. Like an alcoholic taking that first drink and falling off the wagon, if I ate one chocolate egg in a packet, it was easy to eat the rest and buy a new packet to replace it so no one was the wiser.

Now, weight is a funny word, isn't it? We can give weight to an argument, and that is a good thing. We can weigh things up and come to a decision, and that is a good thing too. Sailors can weigh anchor, and somehow everyone is jubilant and tooting horns, throwing streamers, crying, and feeling excited. We can study weighty subjects and be properly proud of our intellectual prowess at our profound understanding of them. We can weigh things down to keep them submerged or stable. We can be weighed down ourselves, none more so than when we weigh more than we want.

I decided I needed to lose weight. Eight months later, although I had lost some six pounds, I was still in serious trouble. My waist was 42.5 inches (108 centimetres), with obesity being marked by a waist larger than 34.6 inches (80 centimetres). I was however, convinced this time I would be successful because I was going to deal with the emotions that precipitated the emotional eating, not simply try to deal with the overeating.

I had lost thirty-eight pounds (seventeen kilograms) on a high-protein diet some years earlier but subsequently regained most of it. I have lost weight going to the gym, going to Weight Watchers meetings, and counting calories. I knew that no matter what program I used, such as the high-protein diet, CSIRO (Commonwealth Scientific and Industrial Research Organisation) Total Wellbeing diet, my dietician's diet, or even hypnosis tapes it was not going to work over the long term if I did not identify the emotional basis for my eating more food than I needed.

> Jacquie's Story
>
> She gained five kilograms over the last six months. She was adamant it was due to her lack of exercise and not the fact that she was eating more than she needed, owing to her anxiety. She was sure that the juice cordial that was replacing her alcohol consumption had to be better than the wine, in terms of lower sugar content. After all, she had free access to cordial as a child, so she reasoned it must have been on the approved parental list of goodies. She was ignoring the fact that a litre of cordial concentrate contains two and a quarter cups of sugar. Her continuing desire for cordial as a replacement for wine was rooted in her childhood memories when it was readily available and acceptable.

Aside from accepting the myth that gaining weight was rather inevitable as I grew older, I had falsely assumed I was not an emotional eater, as this smacked a little too much of lack of control, of weakness and psychological deficit. As a therapist, perhaps one might think I could have countenanced this.

I accepted too much in, not enough out, re: calories (or should I say kilojoules?) but did not see why I would want more going in than I needed. I attended a workshop given by another psychologist on weight loss. This aided my understanding that like everyone else, I too ate to comfort myself.

Gaining weight meant I was eating more than I physically needed. Period. If it wasn't a physical need I was feeding, it had to be an emotional need. If I only focused on the expenditure side of the ledger, believing I had to increase output, I was missing important information about input. I needed to address the idea that I ignored facts if they were counter to my desires.

The grandma in me filled the candy jar, but my inner child, who was not feeling looked after or special, ate the candy! I had to find her and work out why she was eating too much for my body.

I was convinced the reason I was eating more calories than I needed had nothing to do with how many birthdays I had celebrated. Otherwise there would never be a fat kid, would there?

One reason I stored abdominal fat was because I released cortisol in response to stress. We are very primitive. The limbic system's reaction to stress is fight or flight (or freeze). It is designed for our physical survival in a hostile, natural environment of wild animals and few people. It is not designed or well suited for a crowded urban environment in the twenty-first century.

Cortisol readied me to fight or run away. Cortisol had evolved to then initiate hunger to increase consumption of food to replace the energy that should have been expended in fighting and running away. Even though I had not fought or run away, cortisol still initiated hunger to replace the use of energy that had not been used. I needed to identify what was happening that was stressful and caused the release of cortisol. My brain was making me eat, but something else was happening too.

When had emotional eating begun playing a part in my life? I set out to discover what was going on. I was moving well into my personal journey of self-awareness and exploration. I admit it was daunting, even scary, yet I felt reaffirmed, empowered, and ready for major changes in my life. Those changes did come, but it took time and courage to make them happen. I had to investigate my life as if I was telling a therapist.

At seventeen, I enrolled in university weighing seven and a half stone (ninety-eight pounds, or 47.6 kilograms) and standing five foot, five inches (165 centimetres). This gave me a normal BMI for my age of seventeen. I wore my dark brown hair cut short in a feathery style about my face. My hazel eyes were brown with gold flecks, tending to green.

I was myopic but did not wear my glasses as often as I needed. Unfortunately, I had acne all over my face that caused me great distress. My myopia somewhat protected me from how bad my skin actually looked. I imagined in my naïvety that if people were not really close to me, they, like me, would not actually see how bad my skin appeared. After all, if I stepped back from the mirror, I couldn't see the pimples!

Recently, having had recurrent occurrences of what I considered as acne, even in my forties and fifties, my doctor diagnosed a type of dermatitis that is particularly exacerbated by stress. Every time, including when I was a teenager, my episodes of "acne" were always associated with stress.

My skin was olive, and I always had a lovely suntan. I had shapely legs and small feet, nearly as small as my mother's. My face was oval, and I had petite ears without lobes flat against my skull. I have always rather liked my ears, probably because they were like my father's. My eyebrows were plucked to a gentle arch, and I wore no make-up or jewellery. My fingers were slender. I wore my nails gently rounded but unpolished. I was rather proud of my hands, remembering that an aunt had complimented me on them, advising me to always look after my nails. It had been a sad day when a nurse at the hospital, when I was six, cut them very short, admonishing me that I was too young to have long fingernails. No one ever told me I was pretty, but looking at photos, I believe I was. My figure was very slender and somewhat androgynous. It was a worry to me that I was flat-chested.

Five years later, on March 20, 1969, I weighed 119 pounds (54 kilograms), with a BMI 19.8, placing me on the lowest edge of the normal weight range. At 119 "pounds of fun, that's my little honey bun"—a la the song "Honey Bun" from the musical *South Pacific*—I knew I was overweight as she only weighed 101 pounds. When fitted for a bridesmaid dress a year earlier, the dressmaker had remarked on how difficult it was, as I kept getting fatter between fittings. Despite being on the low side of the normal range, I was on a diet to lose weight.

When I married five months later, I weighed 126 pounds (57 kilograms) and was convinced I was fat! This weight actually gave me a BMI of 20.9 and kept me in the normal weight category. I was not fat, though in my twenty-fourth year, my shape had matured. I was no longer androgynous, having developed breasts and wider hips. If I had stayed the same weight I was at seventeen, I would have been considered underweight for my age and height.

My body was a more female shape, but I do not remember that ever being noted by others or myself. In fact, Dan wrote that I should not worry about losing weight if it made me cranky, which I certainly understood implied I was fat. It seems my emotions were also a bother. Ten days before the wedding still worried obviously about how fat I was, I went on an egg and orange diet for a short period to shed a few pounds.

Certainly the weight gain during the engagement indicates emotional eating occurring. There definitely was anxiety around getting married. Looking at it from this distance, I can see that prior to my marriage, I must have used food for comfort.

I am fortunate that I have hundreds of letters between Daniel and me that have assisted me in understanding the formation of our relationship. Not having read the correspondence for forty years, I found it amazing how well they illuminated the later difficulties in my life, difficulties that were already present in those letters. Trying to read them was very hard, and I only dabbled in them for many months, having been overcome by sadness when I first tried.

At the beginning of our relationship, letters were equivocal. Not yet twenty, all I read was that I was loved. However, I soon was writing, "When you kiss me, am I there for you? Do you know I am there?"

After he broke off the relationship three times during those three years, I applied for a teaching transfer and was posted to a small country town hundreds of miles away. I left home to make it easier to forget him. I was very surprised that he began writing to me.

In an early letter, I replied to a suggestion his father made, stating, "It isn't my idea that we should marry because I should be good for you. From what I have seen of marriages, unless both are happy beforehand with being together, I can't see how it can do anything but be worse."

Furthermore, two months later, after he flew up to visit, I wrote, "I'm stupid, aren't I? I don't know what was missing, but you were disappointed so something was.... Perhaps I lack what you want, which I suppose is the point. I suppose too I was under the impression that you knew what you wanted now. It didn't occur to me that this was another testing period. I guess because I knew I'd fail? It hurts to realise I disappointed you so and didn't give you the happiness we both want. I didn't realise I was so successful at repression ... I was afraid to talk. I was afraid I'd hear you say or imply what you in fact did—that you felt differently, that you didn't love me, and I knew I wouldn't be able to overcome that, and I would cry, as I did. Yet it is my fault that you couldn't feel it because I wasn't able to respond quickly enough."

I had learned not to talk about how I was feeling, that indeed I could be quite paralysed, lest I heard I was not good enough to love. I took the blame for any difficulties in the relationship. My emotions were a problem. It was not a good thing if I cried. The ordinary human right of being able to express my emotions was denied me. It seems that in order for him to love me I had to surrender the right to any emotional freedom to express my feelings.

Nevertheless, some three weeks later we became engaged on Holy Thursday, when I flew down for the Easter holidays, and he presented me with an engagement ring. In the airport lounge, he held the little black box in his hand for literally an hour before he gave it to me. He knew I knew it was in his hand and that it would have made me anxious waiting, but I told myself he must have still felt some doubts and I accepted it as understandable. I did not have very good self-esteem and failed to recognise the emotional cost to myself.

When a family member failed to offer marriage to his live-in girlfriend when she wanted to move their relationship up a level so they could start a family, she abruptly left. Regretting his answer, he pursued her, suggesting they marry after all. I admired her stance that if she wasn't good enough to marry yesterday, what had changed to make her good enough to marry today? Unfortunately, in a different era, it never occurred to me. Each time he changed his mind and wanted to resume the relationship, I was hesitant but would be persuaded that he wanted me. I was never confident marriage would happen until it actually did. Even then, I often had dreams during the next ten years when I would awake panicky, confused as to which fiancé I had married.

After becoming engaged, later letters were not more reassuring. On May 25, 1969, I wrote, "Love me? Goodness, I hope you've sent me a more loving letter than the last. Gee, I've been depressed since I received it. … I read a whole lot of your previous letters yesterday. Sometimes you were so tender in your words … and other times sort of bossy or supercilious. Please be loving again, because I love you, and it hurts me when you aren't warm."

I was expecting reciprocity of feelings. I looked hopefully for clues in the letters that my feelings were returned. Was there any emotional eating happening? It seemed pretty conclusive it was happening, as indicated by my weight increasing by six kilograms, or, as I would have known then, by just under fourteen pounds (a stone).

I found the trigger. When I first began emotional eating prior to my marriage, I craved emotional intimacy, that all-encompassing level of warmth and trust; open, intimate communication of thoughts, of feelings, of each other. Criticism, a lack of warmth, and the fear I had yet again disappointed him and that he didn't love me triggered a belief in myself that "I am not good enough." I then engaged in what I would identify more than forty years later as emotional eating. I did not understand that emotional eating would eventually act to suppress the knowledge of what I really felt.

In the 1999 movie *Runaway Bride*, Julia Roberts repeatedly found herself baulking at the altar, suddenly aware she did not want to marry yet another fiancé. I remember being anxious and thinking I should break my engagement, but then surely this was what I had wanted for longer than three years. I thought I was having pre-wedding jitters. I couldn't keep getting engaged and then again break it off! My mother had spent months with Dan planning the wedding. Four years earlier I had broken an engagement that had not entailed any preparations beyond booking a venue, and my mother did not speak to me for six months. My sister was angry with me too. Breaking another engagement was not possible.

On the eve of our wedding, I wrote this poem. The words did not express a lot of confidence, but were quite fearful as I attempted to reassure myself. I created a fantasy for myself, a "happily ever after." My mind then had a task set before it: to protect me from ever having to challenge it. I had been so poetic about it.

> He really loves me, that man does.
> Yet I know not how or why,
> only that tomorrow I'll not despair
> over plans that disappear
> like early dew in the glow of light
> but instead softly envelope me
> in still sunshine.
> I fear not any change, for though
> apart, we are one.

I was not overeating in the first twenty years of my marriage as evidenced by my not experiencing any significant weight gain. With years of calorie-using pregnancies and years of breastfeeding I was not eating more than I needed. Most importantly I enjoyed great self-esteem as a mother, devoting myself to my children. It was in the last eighteen years of marriage that I was overeating.

To explore the emotional connection I had with food, I explored what food meant to me as a child. I could have honed in on the fact that I was bottle-fed from the age of three months and my photos show a too chubby baby, though photos at the age of five show a normal-sized little girl. I believe sometime after the age of two I was still so attached to my "bobble" (bottle) that my mother decided to smash them in front of me, as I obviously was too old to still need them. After all, my sister, fourteen months younger, was using a cup.

A slight sensation in my stomach showed I had an emotional reaction to that. It indicated sadness, but I did not identify this as the most emotionally laden memory at the time. It may be connected to the love of hot cocoa I once consumed before retiring to bed. The memory is preverbal and encoded in my body. Doubtlessly it was a great motivation for my wonderful eleven-year marathon of breastfeeding, albeit with breaks.

This is common when scanning our memories. We tend to remember first those between the ages of five and twelve, but after we process those memories, we can become more in touch with earlier ones.

I sat quietly and thought about my childhood and what relationship I had with food. My mother, I think in shock, saw me one evening, perhaps after a bath, and called me a Belsen horror. Maybe the photos of the survivors from the Bergen-Belsen Nazi concentration camps had been recently released? The photos showed very ill, near-death, emaciated figures.

She was horrified at how skeletal I was and I believe sought to fatten me up. The favourite treat was a cream-filled pastry horn. They did not fatten me up but were probably not a good option for my healthy-weighted sister, who gradually became chubbier throughout childhood. They did increase my liking for fats and sweets and I remembered them with pleasure.

Having decided to work with an EMDR therapist on my emotional eating, once I had identified this memory as the target memory to use with EMDR therapy, we set about disconnecting it from the sense of pleasure with which it was connected, a key procedure in treating any addiction. However, as the standard EMDR protocol focuses on processing traumatic memories, we used a modification known as ICDP (impulse-control disorder protocol) developed by Robert Miller (*Traumatology* 16(3) 2–10).

Miller postulated that specific objects or behaviours link to positive memories, creating a "positive feeling-state."

My specific object was a cream-filled pastry horn. The expected feeling was pleasure. Sitting with the image of the cream-filled pastry horn, the fact that my mother had chosen this as a treat for me reminded me that I was loved. To put it in the usual form for EMDR therapy, "I am loveable." A positive belief or cognition needs to be self-referencing, which is a fancy therapist's way of saying it needs to begin with "I," in contrast to "it" or "you."

The sensations of pleasure in my body related to comfort, fullness in the stomach, a decrease in tension in shoulders, and warmth. I rated this at a six out of ten on the PFS (positive feeling scale) that is used instead of SUDS (subjective units of distress scale). Zero is no positive feeling, with ten being the most intense positive feeling. After using quite a few sets of horizontal eye movements, my PFS was down to zero when I thought about the cream-filled pastry horn.

This was quite successful, and I found it easy to walk past pastries at parties. Despite making lovely baked cheesecakes and other desserts, I found I only wanted to consume a small portion and no longer devoured the rest if any was left uneaten. Even on a cruise down the Danube and Rhine in mid-2012, where there was a smorgasbord of Danish pastries and croissants, I was no longer tempted.

I was armed with more facts and was no longer emotionally attached to pastries, but I continued for another six months to struggle with controlling my eating with minimal success, losing only around six pounds.[4] At the end of 2012 I was still obese at 192 pounds. I needed to go deeper.

Photographs provided me with representations of times when I was overweight. Armed with the conviction now that the only way this could occur was because I was eating more for comfort than to

[4] Loss of 2.5 kilograms and weighing 87.5 kilograms. I had gained twenty kilograms since 1989.

satisfy hunger, I examined my life for the circumstances surrounding those photographs so I could identify the triggers for my needing comfort.

I have a lovely photo of myself from 1989, age forty-two, slender as ever, posing in front of my new kitchen. No irony there? However, by 1994, photographs were far less flattering. In five years, I believe, I gained nearly fifty pounds. I began yoyo dieting, which causes so much trouble to the metabolism. The mantra was that being in my mid-forties, and thus becoming older and possibly perimenopausal, made weight gain normal.

This is an instance of confusing the prevalence of an occurrence (gaining weight by forty-something year olds) as usual, with the concept that it is to be expected as a natural normal part of ageing, which it evidently is not, as women have aged for many millennia, but it is only now we are among the fattest nations on earth.

At this time I was a school guidance officer. Even when working part time, I found taking any break for lunch difficult. Initially appointed to different schools, sometimes changing from one school to another over lunchtime, I found that if I left one school at noon, there was an expectation I should immediately be at the next and ready to work. The staff often gave apologies if a child wasn't available for an interview because he or she had gone out to the playground for lunch!

Even while attending the one campus for the whole day, or even the whole week, there would be such a work load of assessments or interviews that the school had requested that comments would be made by staff if I sat down and had anything to eat: "Lucky for some" if I sat down before the lunchtime bell, or "Don't you have someone to see now?" if I ate during the lunch period, with many comments about how fortunate I was at not having playground duty. However, it was often very difficult to speak to teachers about students if I didn't seek them out during this time, so I always felt I was working, and paying attention to what I ate was not a priority.

> Alison's Story
>
> Alison was a victim of a robbery at her work. Her comfort foods were cakes, derived from her afternoon tea during her primary school years, but her most luscious indulgence was deliciously and slowly eating a Mars Bar during a high school free period. The PFS (positive feeling state) score reduced quite rapidly for eating sugar-coated mangoes: it reduced from seven to zero after eleven sets of eye movements.
>
> During the week she noticed she felt differently about food. However, targeting the healthy choice of strawberries that related to her lifelong love of berries in summer, beginning from crawling into the strawberry patch as an infant, did not remove her pleasure at all.

When I reached home, with children from five years to seventeen, I would be making afternoon teas for the younger ones and be "starving" myself, finding myself eating eight slices of fresh bread and vegemite both before and while making dinner. Several years ago my dietician suggested I needed to find my "feminine appetite" as I had obviously lost it amongst the ravenous appetites of my sons. I knew at the time that the amount of bread I was consuming was not doing me any good and tried unsuccessfully not to eat it. I felt annoyed that I wasn't in control of when I could eat when I was at school. I'd had no problem when I remained at home for twelve years raising my children, despite the amount of stress inherent in that situation of often having no access to money, car, or phone.

In schools, I was rarely able to negotiate a fair situation for myself and sometimes berated myself for my lack of assertiveness. However, my self-esteem was low, and I accepted that I did not have the right to complain. I literally swallowed it. I could teach others to be assertive but not myself. At this point in my journey, I did not understand the reasons for this, or even identify it as a problem. It was something to consider much later.

It was not until I thought about what bread meant to me as a child that I discovered the emotional importance of bread and the basis for my emotional eating originating from that stage of my life. From the age of nine or ten, every afternoon, having walked home from school with my younger sister, we would unlock our house using a complicated set of instructions. We were never given a key, but various keys, like a treasure hunt, allowed us to unlock first one door and then another until we had the backdoor key. We then fetched the money to buy a sixpenny ice-cream cone and a Vienna loaf of bread from the corner shop, some six houses up the street. We cut off the ends of the loaf, scooping out the fresh bread, and generously coated the crust in butter and vegemite (though my sister preferred peanut butter), and refilling the crust with the soft bread, did the same to the top of the slice. Even now I find this thought pleasurable.

I had successfully given up the cream-filled pastry horn that was my first food memory, and such pastries were no longer a problem. However, I still loved fresh bread and struggled with consuming it whenever we baked it ourselves or brought a fresh loaf home. Visiting friends was also a problem, as home-baked bread became a favourite with all of us.

There was an attachment to fresh bread, but what was the emotion? Searching for the importance simply required my looking at the circumstances of when I ate the fresh bread as a child and then as an adult.

As a child, I came home to an empty house and felt I had the responsibility of looking after my younger sister, who often would go play with her friend across the road. We had been told to stay at home.

I ate because I was hungry, but I was also anxious. I was a good girl, but I could not make my sister stay home and be good. I was lonely, as I did not seek out playmates. We were not permitted to have any visitors after school while my mother was at work, and my sister did not play with me.

Talking with my sister over the last two years, she realised she would roam around the street looking for a mother figure. She would opt to play where the mother was present. I never knew about this and assumed she always played with the one friend. We have both wondered what our mother was thinking, as we have ensured never leaving our children unattended, preferring to be there for them until they were independent, at least into their late teens.

I asked my mother some years before her death about the fact that we were "latchkey children" from when we were only ages ten and nine. She told me, "But you were good girls," as if that excused leaving us unattended from six thirty in the morning until six at night. She was a factory worker. To put it in context, she had lost her mother to stomach cancer when she was only seven and her mother forty-seven. She always spoke of raising herself like Topsy from Harriet Beecher Stowe's *Uncle Tom's Cabin.* I don't believe she knew very much about the character, as Topsy was a wild and uncivilised slave girl.

It seemed that if we were well behaved, there was no need for my mother to be there. She had very little empathy for me, though I don't know whether she knew I spent every afternoon alone while my sister was playing elsewhere. Indeed, it wasn't until after her death when I read the journals she wrote in her sixties where she expressed some concern for me that I felt she even acknowledged the distress I must have experienced through my hospitalisations between the ages of six and seven, hospitalisations that meant I was left feeling abandoned and alone.

My main concern was that having recovered my svelte shape yet again, having at this time of writing lost forty-nine pounds (twenty-two kilograms), I did not want to succumb to emotional eating ever again. Simply identifying the connection between food and pleasure was insufficient to disconnect the strong feelings of wanting to eat something I did not need.

I undertook a self-directed EMDR therapy session on the fresh Vienna bread. I was surprised that I rated as high as six out of ten on the positive feeling scale (PFS). My positive belief was "I am safe." After using only a dozen sets of eye movements, my PFS was down to zero when I thought about the bread.

I disconnected pleasure from two types of comfort food: pastries and fresh bread, but I was aware there were other occasions where I overate, such as at parties or situations where food is unlimited, at a banquet setting in a restaurant, or at home with family gatherings that include nibbles and bowls of food I have placed around the house. It was harder to refuse if a family member who'd cooked the food offered it.

I rationalized my brain was hardwired to respond this way because of the feast/famine experience of our hunter/gatherer ancestors. I followed advice to take a plate and put on it that which I wanted to eat. I did have a choice, and if I was not eating for physical needs, because I had not been starved, then I was eating for emotional needs. In a restaurant, I did not go with the prevailing vote to have a banquet, as I knew I ate more than I physically needed. However, as sharing food involves satisfying other social and emotional needs, I have found that if I satisfy these needs with conversation and emotional connection, I am not subjecting myself to emotional eating and find the banquet option viable.

Just as I undertook investigating with pastries and bread, I examined these situations for any pleasure connected to earlier memories of food, which brought up occasions of being a five-year-old flower girl at a wedding and my tenth birthday party. Sitting with these memories, I found there was a sparkle in my eyes, a smile, a sort of preening, and a belief I am special. I feel happy and am smiling. There was no scene for the wedding, but there were the same feelings connected to my tenth birthday party. There were plates of food on the table, and I was allowed to eat whatever I wanted—lollies, chips—and to go back for more. An ice-cream cake was brought out too, with candles and Happy Birthday written on it.

Possibly because of previous work, but self-directed EMDR therapy with a horizontal eye movement very quickly resolved from a PFS score of seven down to zero.

A third pleasure of feeling special is connected with the plates of nibbles found at large gatherings and indeed any social occasion.

Thus three "food types"—pastries, fresh bread, and nibbles—result in three respective positive beliefs: I am loveable, I am safe, and I am special.

Feeding my children by breastfeeding in a very natural way, with demand feeding and baby-led weaning, what I provided for my babies and toddlers was the best nutrition possible. It was not restricted but was demanded by the infant, as nature intended.

Providing food became connected to my self-concept of being a good mother. The problem with being a good mother is whether or not anyone can be good enough. Being good enough was entwined with providing food.

Food is an important part of belonging in our family. So much so that all my children are excellent cooks, once vying for praise on a Sunday when they took turns at providing a delicious meal for up to twenty people, with great expectations of quantity and quality of meats, vegetables, breads, salads, desserts, and beverages.

Furthermore, it became connected to my being a good hostess. All of my in-laws (Daniel is one of nine) were due to arrive on Boxing Day some years ago. I baked nine different desserts so everyone would have their favourite for afternoon tea. Needless to write it, but there were a lot of leftovers.

Working It Through

Is there a problem?

Female: Overweight—waist over 31.5 inches (80 cm).
Obese—waist over 34.6 inches (88 cm)
Male: Overweight—waist over 37 inches (94 cm).
Obese—waist over 40 inches (102 cm)
Calculate your BMI (body mass index). Is it under 25?

Divide your weight by your height squared. The maths teacher in me loves writing that! Or visit the National Heart, Lung, and Blood Institute for a BMI calculator: http://www.nhlbi.nih.gov/health/educational/lose_wt/BMI/bmicalc.htm.

Can you see your toes? No? You are obese.

Can you see your pubic hair? Yes? You are a normal weight.

Find Your Problem

For which foods do you reach? Which foods hold the most attraction? To help you find the answers if you are not sure now, over the next few days or weeks, note what and when you eat, whether you are hungry, and what has been happening to your body. What are you saying to yourself? Are there any emotions or body sensations connected with the experience?

Then sit quietly and recreate the scene. Note the sensations in your body. Have you developed family traditions and celebrations that support your overindulgence in food? Be honest. What foods do you overeat? What secret little habits do you have about which there may be a guilty laugh? Like one of my clients, do you have a childhood memory of lovely, fresh-buttered bread you then dipped in sugar when Mum wasn't looking? Is there a problem season for you like my Christmas and Easter?

Were you rewarded when you ate?

The reward may have been overt praise or expectation.

Are you rewarded by providing food?

Choose a creative way of exploring connections. Perhaps drawing an image of a food, or place, or event will connect and stimulate your childhood neural networks. You might choose to write about a food, a memory, or a thought and develop that by writing down whatever occurs to you, thus journaling about it. Another way is to simply sit, relax, focus on a thought, meditate, and let your mind follow that path, but remember to journal it afterward. Similarly, you could visualise a scene and let it unfold to explore your core negative belief.

When did emotional eating occur? How old were you? What was happening around you each time emotional eating became a problem? It is likely to have occurred more than once.

Now find the foods in which you took particular pleasure as a child. Note the physical pleasure you feel remembering that food.

Note the emotions connected with that physical sensation. Notice the positive belief you held about yourself as a result.

Disconnect the pleasure from the experience of eating that food using EMDR therapy, meditating, or journaling. You will know the method you chose worked if you are no longer tempted with those foods.

You could access help using Robert Miller's modification of EMDR therapy through contacting an EMDR therapist (visit http://emdraa.org).

How many times have you gone on a weight-loss diet?

Visiting the Lifeline Book Fair,[ii] I noted rows and rows of books devoted to weight loss. I didn't have any of them amongst my wide selection at home but was not tempted to buy any of them. How many books are on your shelves, and how often do you go to the food/health/dieting section in bookshops?

Chapter 3

THE GENESIS OF EMOTIONAL EATING

Having identified three foods that I used for emotional eating, I knew I was on my way. I knew which positive beliefs I associated with each food, and I knew the foundation for my emotional eating came from my childhood. To move further, I needed to know more about the reasons I was how I was, so I plunged even deeper into my psyche.

As the EMDR therapy session with my psychologist occurred prior to a three months holiday and she was not immediately available for follow-up through that year, I continued on my own to uncover all the factors involved in my emotional eating. I had discovered the positive feelings of "I am loveable," "I am safe," and "I am special." My task now was to find the negative childhood feelings and beliefs that were necessary for the development of the positive feeling states. Without a desperate need to feel better as a child, there would have been no need to have these special positive feelings.

The obvious choices for those negative feelings were the negatives of what I gained from the comfort foods, of being unlovable, unsafe, and unimportant. For me, those beliefs distilled into one core belief: that I was not good enough.

In order to discover that belief, I became mindful of what I was actually doing in the present. The first clue was noticing the emotional eating that was happening. I had been eating some rice biscuits. My dietician told me I could eat six as a snack. Twelve is double that, and twenty? They are fairly innocuous, aren't they? Yet I had eaten a meal recently, and I was not hungry. I noticed the chatter going on in my head about the emotional eating.

Earlier I was aware I was feeling anxious. This was the emotion.

I had decided I would not contact a friend. I was not sure I would receive the reassurance I knew I wanted. This was the precipitating event.

There was a sensation in my throat of discomfort, fuzziness in my head, a tension down the spine, a hunching of the shoulders. These were the sensations in my body that were the precursors to my emotional eating.

Examining another scenario, I noted the emotion of feeling anxious. Many years ago I could not locate my three-year-old daughter. She had been playing with her brother and friends next door. I raced around the neighbourhood searching, enlisting all I could. After what seemed a long time I returned home distraught only to find her asleep in the bed where I had put her. I then remembered I had fetched her from next door to put her down for a nap. I felt very embarrassed that I could forget where my child was. After telling a friend about this episode I became anxious. I was fearful that my friend might cease to hold me in good regard. Perhaps she would not talk with me anymore. I felt the bodily sensations of the catch in my breath, the tightness in my chest, the constriction in my throat, tension across the back of my shoulders, and fuzziness in my head. I then so wanted to eat!

Having noted the above two occasions where I experienced an impulse to eat for comfort, the physical symptoms were very similar. Closing my eyes, I imagined those symptoms and that feeling of anxiety and allowed myself to go back through the years. I floated back, concentrating on those bodily sensations to times when I had experienced them before.

The first memory that came to mind was where a neighbour had told my mother that my sister was on the side of the road with her friend, an elastic band stretched across the road between them, pinging cars. Of course she was supposed to be home with me.

Dad was a very handsome man, with darkly tanned skin gained from his hours outdoors as a deliveryman for a large national chain of departmental stores. He resembled the 1950s actor Rory Calhoun with his very blue eyes, dark, thick curly hair, and six-foot, one-inch frame.

Arriving home late from working overtime, after we were asleep, our father came into our shared bedroom. I woke to see him lift the blankets, raise his hand to the ceiling, and bring it down hard on her bare bottom as her nightgown had ruffled up, leaving her buttocks exposed. I was terrified. I felt responsible. It was my fault. I should have done something. It was quite frightening being woken to that scene. I did not feel safe.

Spanking was not a common occurrence. I remember only one time being chased into the closet by my father, who was angry and threatening. My mother was the usual disciplinarian, wielding the cane handle of the feather duster on more than one occasion. My sister and I laughed once about the fact that for a number of years we actually saved up our measly pocket money to buy a feather duster as a Mother's Day present. Age eleven, for the first and only time in my life, I received a smack across my face from the back of mother's hand, for the impudence of closing my eyes when she spoke to me. It was a low level of physical abuse well tolerated and expected in the era.

When I processed this memory of waking to see my father hitting my sister, using bilateral eye movements, I felt the constriction in my throat and discomfort in my stomach. My negative cognition was "I am not safe," and my preferred positive cognition was "I am okay," with a validity score of five out of seven, meaning I nearly believed it.

It startled me that I could feel this distress when the memory was sixty years old and my father had been dead for twenty years. There was no way I was unsafe or could realistically fear I was about to be spanked by him. I knew it was important to notice that the feeling was as if it were now, in the present. I noticed my language changed as the memory was processed. The tense in which I thought and spoke began to change from the present to the past.

My SUDS was seven out of ten. This was a high level of distressed. The immediate thoughts that surfaced were around not being able to protect my sister, being powerless, and how it was best not to go outside, to be good in order to remain safe. I felt highly responsible for my sister and was very anxious.

Continuing to focus on the bodily sensations and the emotion of anxiety, a second memory came to mind. My teacher's laced-up shoes were the first things I saw. I was sitting at my desk in school, very thin, very anxious, my head bent forward as I read the list of spelling words on my lap. I didn't know how to spell anything, or so it seemed. I don't remember having spelling tests at my previous school. I was six-and-a-half years old.

I was sitting alone at one of those old-fashioned desks for two children, with the seat attached to the desk. I had moved schools. I had not been to school for a couple of months, having been hospitalised, as I had been very sick with scarlet fever. My family had been told not to visit me, as it would only upset me, so I had spent ten days looking at the little window at the end of the ward, hoping to see my parents' faces. My family had moved to our new house while I was convalescing, and I did not return to my school to farewell my friends.

Miss Stubbs yelled at me for cheating and told me to stay in the corner of the classroom and not look at any of the other children. When it came time for "little lunch," I walked out last and didn't know where the toilet block was, so I wet my pants.

I never articulated that I wasn't good enough when I was a child. Children don't. Children blame themselves in black and white terms: I am good; I am bad. I tried very hard to be a good child. I didn't feel I was good enough. I couldn't speak up and say it was unjust or unfair, that I wasn't there last week when she gave out the spelling homework. I couldn't say, "But I'm the new kid here, I don't know the rules." I didn't know about the Broca's area in the brain that controls speech being down-lit as the amygdala is activated so it makes it literally harder to speak.

This was not the last time I would be dumbstruck when I was under attack. When people criticized me, I found myself unable to find the words to defend myself. When I felt anxious or ashamed, I would retreat into silence. I have been told I have a little "fake-it-till-you-make" laugh that is a telltale sign of my nervousness.

I was humiliated and shamed. People showed me disgust, as firstly I had cheated, secondly I was stood all day in the corner of the classroom, and thirdly I had wet my pants. I remember only ever having one friend at my new school and being very lonely on the playground all through my primary years. I was anxious, lacked confidence, and felt isolated and unwanted.

Another incident came to mind as I focused on the bodily sensations. Fourteen years later, I found myself telling a lie to my closest friend on her wedding day. It was a devastating moment. Her face was framed in her white veil. Her eyes sparkled with excitement and happiness as she told me it would be my turn soon. I couldn't tell her that the relationship had finished two days earlier. I couldn't let her know that later when she saw him at her wedding reception, he would only be pretending to be with me.

I still felt guilty, even though to have told the truth would have made her feel sad, and I couldn't do that. I was anxious she would see through me but now realise I was already adept at hiding my feelings from other people. The problem was I became as skilled at hiding my feelings from myself.

There I was, age sixty-six, and my core belief of "I am not good enough" had resulted in my overeating for twenty years. This was somewhat shocking. I perceived myself as a loving wife, mother, grandmother, great-grandmother, sister, aunt, friend, and daughter, a caring, competent professional and a committed member of my church. I was all those things, but it did not mean I always felt like I was a loved wife, a loved mother, a loved grandmother, great-grandmother, sister, aunt, or friend or that others saw me as a competent professional and committed member of my parish. As I focused on my responsibilities to be caring and loving, I ignored when I did not feel I was cared for and loved.

I had projected this outwardly so successfully that friends and family discovering how I have felt underneath have been shocked and dismayed. This is understandable, as these feelings were not often in my conscious awareness either. In the earlier years, I took long showers and if upset, was in tears during them. I was told I was wasting water and asked if I was ever going to get out of the shower, so I effectively stopped this emotional outlet. I swapped my long hot showers with overeating.

A motley of beliefs surfaced around the weight of responsibility that was assuaged by fresh bread, butter, and vegemite. It was my responsibility that things worked well for my children, my spouse, my clients, and my friends, as it was my responsibility to keep my sister safe. If anything went wrong, I often believed I should have done something. I never thought I had done the best I could. It is a wonder I stopped at a dress size twenty with all that to carry.

When I have felt I was not good enough, fresh bread filled the bill. When I was lonely, fresh bread brought me the feelings of being loveable, of being good enough. When I felt unsafe, anxious, a slice of white bread fresh from the oven, a dinner roll, and other varieties from a specialty bakers' shop, or even toasted raisin bread all connected with feelings of safety, of being okay, of being good enough.

A fear can generalise so that anything furry becomes a trigger for anxiety as could happen if as a child you were terrified of Santa Claus. Pleasurable events can generalise too. Raisin toast brings me the memory and feelings of being with a dear friend during university, sitting in the women's union, drinking coffee, and chatting. Dinner rolls are especially associated with times with friends in restaurants or at each others' homes. Buying bread from a specialty shop obviously resonates with a feeling of a special occasion, but for me the memory is one of buying a grandchild a cheese and bacon roll when I minded him when he was a preschooler. Fresh home-baked bread permeates my soul with good feelings. There were connections from childhood foods to ones I was over-consuming.

If things went awry when I was responsible, a corollary was I was afraid I was not good enough because this was how it played out in my childhood. Then I reached for food. This became automatic. It was similar to when I learned to drive a car and no longer had to concentrate in order to steer and change gears at the same time. I was no longer consciously aware of what negative feelings I felt and had developed habits to deal with the emotions that were connected to foods which were associated with positive feelings. One can learn to pay careful attention again to the mechanics of driving. I needed to be mindful about eating and what had motivated me to consume food when I was not hungry.

Dreams showed me my brain was mulling over my problems. My mind tried to show me what I was feeling when I stopped paying attention to how I felt. It could only convey its message in symbols and images that I had to decipher. I have recorded my dreams intermittently for longer than twenty years.

One in 1992 shows a conflict between two parts of myself, for indeed, in a dream, one can interpret the dream from the perspective that every part belongs to the dreamer. I reproduce it largely the way I wrote it.

July 15, 1992: I was in a square room seen from above by someone, stuck on a chair that could be pushed around the room. I was moving it around the room with my feet pushing against the floor. My abductor was near me, not really pushing the chair, more like following it. I was not able to really escape him, being stuck to the chair, and then he was threatening me. The person looking down came through the skylight and my abductor leapt up, touching the walls, the ceiling like a spider, and I ran out the door.

I ran to the car. I could only open the back passenger door on the left side, parked nearest the building—it was wooden, old. The back of the car had a big square based box, tall, filling the seat. I shoved it across. By then my kidnapper had come out and pushed me across. He drove the car from that back left passenger seat. I leaned behind him, opened the door, and shoved him out of the car. He ran with the door open, steering the car with his fingertips just touching the steering wheel.

I opened my car door and ran along holding on, but it was going too fast. I grabbed and jerked the steering wheel, and he couldn't hold on. I let go and ran, rolling in the grass, safe. The car crashed into a pole, denting it badly. I assumed he was dead, or injured.

I ran back to a house—big tall Queenslander sort of house—went to the front door, but no answer; big brown door with a big brass knocker. But I could hear music inside—the Beatles' "Love Me Do." I went downstairs and around the back. A big wire mesh fence came off the house to the back, parallel to the driveway. I opened the tall mesh gate. A big dog—thin, pointed snout, long shaggy, golden-brown hair—came toward me. I saw my abductor walk past the front of the house looking for me. I crouched down in long, long grass. Either he or I had a very bright, multicoloured shirt on. I didn't think he saw me. The woman was beside me still. I told her my story.

A woman, washed-out blonde, longish hair, shoulder length, rough-looking, came next to me. "He won't hurt you." She told me her story. She was waiting for her boyfriend, and I asked her for help, protection.

I went inside to phone, but I couldn't find the phone. Then I went into the front bedroom. I opened the door. The walls, woodwork, everywhere were pale, creamy.

He was in there: so was the woman. I said, "Why, why didn't you believe me?"

She said, "Why not? You believed me and it was a lie."

I tried to phone, but I couldn't get through. They didn't try to stop me. They didn't need to.

If one assumes in a dream that every part is oneself, I guess I tried to tell me but didn't get through! I don't remember analyzing the dream at the time. Using transpersonal concepts, the person looking through the skylight could be interpreted as my "higher self". This dream predated the emotional eating that was about to begin. My abductor scared off my "higher self". I had recently ceased attending the Charismatic Mass conducted by my parish priest. I was told such masses were too emotional and that religion should be based on an intellectual assent. I was aware that attending them might put great pressure on my marriage.

Sitting on a chair is something one does to relax but I could not relax. There was too much to do. I had felt stuck, pushed around, manipulated, but I had escaped from the situation. I had completed my postgraduate studies and was working full-time. Yet I was still not in control of my life. I did not get into the driver's seat but into the passenger's seat, from which I was dislodged and I was steered (symbolically the car represented my physical self) with very little pressure on the steering wheel with fingertips, even after I pushed him out. Then I ran alongside too, remaining in the situation where he was controlling my life until there was a crisis.

Without attempting a complete dream analysis, unanswered doors as missed opportunities or lack of response for help, and not being able to find a phone so I was not able to communicate with anyone seem fairly obvious. This mirrored my life, though dreams make more sense a long time afterward, it seems to me now! Perhaps it made sense then too. A teenage pregnancy, my father's death, a suicide, severe asthma and financial difficulties and other crises were more important than me, or so I chose at that time, but this dream that followed these occurrences warned me of the consequences of my choice.

It resonated with me when Queen Elizabeth II described 1992 as her "annus horribilis". This was another pivotal year in my life. The emotional time bomb fashioned in the jungles of Borneo and New Guinea wrought further destruction. My father's final rejection played out in the last six months of his life when he refused to speak with me. I was there at his deathbed as he lay heavily sedated, sad we had never reconciled. My sister informed me he had told her I had failed him in allowing his granddaughter to become pregnant.

Before separating from Daniel in mid-2013, I dreamed I had woken up thinking I had not put in my assignments. I have not been able to work out when the maths classes I was teaching were on and have missed them for seven weeks. The assignment for sociology was due the day before. I felt panic; I was going to fail my degree.

The reality was I never took sociology! I haven't taught mathematics for thirty years! I hadn't been studying and submitting assignments either. I also realised this was not a new dream.

Did it have any meaning?

Perhaps I was worried I wasn't doing what I had made a commitment to do and other people were relying on me. The commitments were long-standing. They seemed to indicate failure. Commitments to have and to hold, for better or worse, in sickness and in health were being challenged.

I could delve deeper, and search out the meaning of seven, for instance. The seven days of the week, the seven deadly sins, or even the seven chakras may appeal. It may refer to the size of my family, or the house number of our first home.

Looking at assignments, the thought is that it is a task given to you by another, as a means of qualifying for or earning something. Assignments aren't joy-filled pursuits and indeed appear to have no appeal. The question was, were there tasks others had assigned to me that I was not completing? A resounding yes reverberated in my head.

I wondered if I didn't want to do housework, cook, or do any of the mundane tasks around the house. Maybe I no longer wanted to allow my life to be bound by expectations of housework and gardening, cooking and cleaning. This did not ring completely true. I loved a clean house and to cook an apple pie or a cheesecake, to have guests and play hostess. I enjoyed planting and pruning. There were tasks, though, that I didn't want and hadn't chosen. It was going to take many months for this to become clearer.

Impromptu barbeques with young children and neighbours on a Sunday afternoon had evolved into an elaborate family ritual of eating and drinking. Fiancées would demur that they were now expected to spend every Sunday afternoon with their future-in-laws. Siblings put pressure on each other to participate. Staying at home and chilling out were not acceptable as reasons for not attending. Comments were made and questions asked if someone didn't appear.

With adult children, their partners, families, and friends, it was not unusual to have more than twenty people in the gazebo in summer, swimming and showering before and after dinner. In winter rooms were rearranged every weekend with trestle tables to seat them all. This entailed a great deal of preparation and clearing away. Where once it had all been a shared experience with Daniel, I realised I now shouldered much of the post-party work on my own.

The challenge of understanding dreams was the need to continue. What was the significance in my dream of my teaching maths? It was such a long time ago, and I would not be able to do it now, nor would I be interested in it. Then I noticed a visceral reaction. I completed my training to teach maths forty-five years ago. I would not know how to teach it today. I would not want to do that today. I was passionate about it then but would be bored to tears with it now. It also seemed to me other things I was passionate about no longer interested me. Indeed, a happy afternoon on a Sunday in the 1980s with my young children and neighbours contrasted with how I felt with the present reality.

Sociology quickly related to society and my not meeting the expectations of society. I was soon to find that the societal expectations I was going to fail to meet were those of my children, as I could no longer play "happy families" and present a perfect image for them. I was afraid my friends and colleagues, and extended family would be disappointed too, but their understanding was not clouded as was that of my children, as they understood far more than I.

Various female friends and relatives acknowledged things they had noticed but had assumed that even though it would not have suited them, they chose to say nothing, as I seemed content. One close friend stated she had instituted a similar family gathering every week only to find within a month she and they had tired of it.

Searching the meaning of seven, the attainment of high spirituality flattered me. It may refer to a seven-year-itch type of rut and need for change, or as a sign of conflict. It is rather pleasant reading that it indicates things are anything but ordinary, but that seemed like the supposedly Chinese curse of living in interesting times. Completeness seems to be another meaning. The seventh house in astrology rules marriage.

Concerns about my unhealthy weight led me to uncover and address my core negative belief of not being good enough. My dreams revealed I was aware of the unsatisfactory nature of my everyday reality in my roles as wife, mother and grandmother. I did not fully recognise then what my dreams were trying to communicate, but they were showing me the way through a half-opened door.

In another dream I had not long afterward, a big, baggy, square-necked, trapezium of a tunic-shaped dress, the bottom much wider than the top, with wide, three-quarter sleeves, was made for me by a friend. I think this reflected my concern about my weight and how people perceived me.

What Did I Feel in My Body When I Thought about These Dreams?

Twenty years later I reconnected with the first dream and considered recent ones. I scanned my body to note what was happening in it in reaction to my thinking about these dreams. Moving my attention from the top of my head down to my toes, I noticed my ears hurt. I relaxed myself, slowing down my breathing, noting that I had no abscess in my ears. I had not been affirmed. No one came to stroke my forehead. As I made these connections, focusing on my body, contemplating the meaning of my dreams, and noting what memories arose, I was able to recognise how the core belief of not being good enough had affected my life and relationships.

Certainly during my childhood I had not been as confident as I may have appeared. I strove for excellence academically in high school, but in my personal relationships, I was and remained lonely and unable to communicate at any intimate level. Developmentally this is understandable. My close girlfriends and former classmates relate to these feelings. We saw each other as having more confidence than we actually possessed.

At my fortieth school reunion, a classmate said she always admired me very much for my intelligence and appearance. I couldn't believe it. I had nearly not gone. I did not like my appearance and felt ashamed at being so overweight. I worried what they would think when they found out I had so many children and grandchildren.

People had often made comments about whether or not I knew what caused pregnancy. I wondered what they would think about my having converted to Catholicism and very nearly convinced myself not to attend. I had not kept in touch with anyone since we had graduated from high school in 1963.

Her perception of me still doesn't accord with how I remember thinking about myself. I had no inkling she even really liked me much, despite my wanting to be friends! We never went to each other's house, and we could not phone each other, as I had no phone at home. We only saw each other at school.

Yet as distressing memories have been processed I have become more aware of playing, chatting and enjoying the company of classmates throughout my school years. This is the usual result of processing negative memories. It allows the positive ones to surface. We built cubby houses out of the mown grass at school, by stacking the hay as walls. When I was in high school I often delighted in drawing house plans reminiscent of this activity. We played doctors and nurses, taking turns to lie down on the playground bench and pretend to have our temperatures taken and bandages applied. We practised folk dancing and formation marching. It is a great pleasure realising that once the negative has been dealt with I can see the positive.

Ten years later, at the fiftieth reunion, I very diffidently considered whether to inform them I had left Dan after forty-three years of marriage. Their reaction was one of support and encouragement. My former classmates were astounded that I had self-esteem issues throughout my whole life. They recognised that I was never told how well I had done because it seemed so obvious there appeared no need. Even now this sounds extremely strange to me.

After another two years we met again, no longer willing to allow a decade between reunions since we were aware not all of us would be alive to attend the next one. Delving more deeply, we realised that we each walked around in our own little bubbles, imagining that our lives were all the same. Where one had a close supportive relationship with her father, she imagined we all had. We understandably projected our own childhood experiences onto each other. Coupled with the admonition against talking about family matters outside of the home, unlike later generations, baby boomers had little experience of intimate school friend conversations.

However, being reminded of some of the high jinx in what we were involved has more accurately coloured my high school years. Disconnecting from them when I left school prevented the normal memorisation of our friendships that could include playing up on a teacher in first year and planning a wonderful "muck-up" day at the end of fifth and all the other episodes of teenage girls interacting and learning about themselves and others.

My parents gave no affirmation concerning my grades, being top of my year, being first in any subject, not even when I was the dux of the school. I didn't even try to shine at university. What was the point? The teacher I most admired at my high school had told me I would be a little fish in a big pond and that I shouldn't expect to be able to compete as well as I had at school. Years later I learned about the damage that could be done to their academic success when teachers were given false information about how intelligent students were. I had not realised how her self-fulfilling prophecy had affected me.

After we moved from Perth, regular visits back to visit both Dan's and my parents resulted in my often feeling so dejected and sad that I needed a lot of positive self-talk to improve my mood. My father was very critical. Within twenty minutes of arriving, he would complain about the mess we had made in the house. He disliked the number of bags and toys that my family needed. I never felt truly welcomed by him. I was very aware that our visits incommoded him. I told myself that as an adult, I didn't need to know my father loved me, as Dan, my children, and my friends did. Of course, none of the positive self-talk really healed the hurt. It only made me feel better for a while. Worse still, it set me up to be dependent on the regard of others to maintain my self-worth. I had substituted the need to seek the approval of Dan, children, friends, colleagues, managers, and even volunteer organisations and associations for my need for my parents' approval that I never felt I gained.

I was not good at accepting compliments or help, as underneath the external confidence I did not quite believe I was good enough or worthy of receiving a compliment or assistance. If someone complimented me, such as a student welfare teacher telling me I was the best school counsellor with whom she had ever worked, I had no way of accepting the compliment. I felt embarrassed, probably because I thought she must have not known how really pathetic I was. Even when a friend wanted to give me something as helpful as a prepared casserole to assist me when Dan was immobilised following a car accident (see chapter 6 for more information), and I was about to give birth to my fifth child, I rejected her offer. Years later she told me this rejection had been keenly felt.

Shame

However, another feeling state is created after emotional eating, usually shame and guilt, when the emotional eating has resulted in other symptoms, most obviously—for me—being overweight or unhealthy. Reflux, high cholesterol, and asthma were involved. I needed to lose weight. I felt terribly guilty whenever I succumbed to emotional eating. Guilt is the common emotion anyone feels after indulging in addictive behaviour, and it cycles back into causing more of the same, which for me was more overeating. Guilt follows the behaviour. Guilt and shame are collaborative emotions. This then resulted in even more emotional eating, as I wasn't even good enough to lose weight!

The additional feelings of being inadequate were particularly burdensome. How could I be so overweight and claim to be a good therapist when it was obvious I was not dealing with my own issues? It reminded me of the nurse who counselled me after a mammogram about the need to maintain an appropriate weight. At the time I had lost the weight, but she sat uncomfortably on her chair, her weight unsupported. She looked much heavier than I had ever been. My lack of comment to her reinforced the fact that my clients would have noticed but also would not have commented. The message is very much influenced by the messenger! She, as I, was not able to demonstrate the wisdom of her words.

What was stopping us being able to behave in accordance with our beliefs? Surely if we believed them, we would not be sitting there in front of clients in physically obvious contradiction. Beliefs around it being normal to get fatter as I aged were rationalisations that protected me from the truth that overeating was an emotional issue that as a therapist I ought to have addressed. However at any meeting of psychologists, I was not alone in having weight issues though I promise my colleagues I never attempted to take a tally.

I found I had to broaden the concept of emotional eating beyond the intake of food. All the dieting, exercise, and use of strategies to boost my willpower, all the books I read about nutrition and downloads from the internet on cuisine all entailed a huge amount of time and effort so that even when I was triggered by the belief that "I was not good enough" and did not eat, my concentration on strategies to prevent me overeating had the exact same effect—that of masking the triggering belief of being inadequate. Visiting the gym, going for walks, writing out lists of things to do instead of eating, seeing a dietician, joining a programme, listening to tapes, keeping a food diary, downloading an app for my iPhone to count calories (kilojoules), recording exercise, and all the rest were simply brilliant strategies that prevented me from even knowing what was so wrong.

I could not identify what was wrong until I stopped emotionally eating and ceased being engaged in all the distracting paraphernalia of dieting. I no longer wanted to eat my comfort foods, as they no longer gave me the comfort they once gave me. I could now recognise that prior to doing this work, I would have gone to the pantry or engaged in things to distract and avoid eating, such as select an item from a list of things I could during such a time. Drinking an ice-cold tumbler of water, cleaning a cupboard, sorting a sock drawer, or any of a hundred things could have been given priority to eating. I emphasise "could" because it was not possible beforehand to actually notice the triggering belief.

This is the hard part of the journey. This is what my mind was protecting me from examining. Many people do not take as long as I did to recognise the problem, but hiding it from myself lasted twenty years.

The Other Side of the Coin

By examining my life for periods when I was not emotionally eating, I was able to gain greater clarity. When I did not need to eat for reasons other than my physical needs, because my emotional needs were being met, it became even more apparent that I was too dependent upon the approval of others rather than holding an inner sense of worthiness. Many times I was fine.

Throughout my life there were many years where I knew I was capable and worthy. In fourth grade, because I was a good reader I was chosen to run a group for third graders who needed to practise their reading. We would take our chairs out into the playground to form a circle. I checked their names off the list as they read. At fourteen I was a Sunday school teacher, reading the Bible stories to the group of five-year-olds each week. I replicated this when I instigated Children's Liturgy during the Reading of the Word at Mass.

Pregnancy, birthing, and lactation were easy for me. My body worked for me, and I learned to trust it. As a mother running playgroups, as a local leader for the CWL (Catholic Women's League), as one of its state presidents, as a member of the school and parish board and on school committees, as a student earning my master's when I had a family to raise, I enjoyed many years of good self-esteem. As a result, I was not eating emotionally and was unaware of the core belief of "I am not good enough" that lay lurking just out of the awareness of my conscious mind. Looking at these and other times, a common thread is that others noted my competence and told me.

The question is, how, at sixty-six, did I suddenly recognise this core belief of "I am not good enough"? How is it possible? Looking at what the triggers were and when they were not present, there is a lack of affirmation and negative comment.

Current Triggers

What are the triggers happening now? Keeping a diary was very helpful as it helped highlight where the triggers existed.

> April 3, 2013: I have lost forty-six pounds (twenty-one kg), and I bought size ten pants today, down from size eighteen. There have been no congratulations about looking fabulous, but there are comments that I have lost my *ugly bits*. I have donated a huge amount of clothes to charity because I am not fat enough to fill them out. I do not eat my share of food left over from family gatherings. I made soup from the home-grown squash and leeks but did not eat it. Nor did I eat the Sunday cooked ham, or leftover meat from the leg of lamb from the Holy Thursday dinner six nights ago. As well I threw out the mint peas from Sunday. I thought one and a half kilos (three pounds) of peas was overdoing it. "Waste not, want not" is not my favourite saying. I was tired of hearing it. Funny about the peas: as an eight-year-old I was forced to sit for two hours until I finally gave in and ate my very by-then cold peas.

I wanted to eat something sweet or fresh bread, but I chose to journal rather than do what I obviously once would have. Even going for a walk, which many a time was an option and seemingly so much healthier, also served as a distraction from the emotions I did not want to experience. I felt angry, disgusted, devalued.

I don't want to eat food I don't need. I would rather be an appropriate weight and healthy. It was interesting how I framed this to myself, like a rebellious child, being told to eat her veggies because the children in China are starving. I began choosing what I wanted to eat and when and in response to what my body told me, rather than to what circumstances dictated.

I felt sadness around my eyes and mouth, a lump in my throat, a panicky feeling in my chest, a fear of loneliness flooding me. Normally I would have fetched something to eat!

Each day I wanted only a small piece of fish but was told the ham that had been defrosted must be consumed, but I asserted "not by me." I was not really that interested in eating ham. Very recently, I would have given in to the fact that it would be a waste not to eat the ham, despite not wanting to eat ham for many years. My dietician was not enamoured of pork at all.

*

> May 25, 2013: I have lost twenty-five kilos (fifty-one pounds), the level of cholesterol has improved (good cholesterol is higher, but the overall number remains 6.0, a healthy range), and protein in urine is reduced, so kidney function is better.

I bought a couple of jackets, and was told I would have to breathe in, as they looked a bit small. They weren't at all, as I demonstrated. I went into Dan's study to find him buying another piece for his collection. It didn't cost much more than my two jackets. I have become very aware of the negative comments directed at me. Now it seemed to me that there were financial consequences.

Several months after writing this, I cooked whatever I wanted, even if a dish was being reheated that I did not want to share. I had lost fifty-five pounds (twenty-five kilograms), despite travelling abroad where weight gain could have been an easy result of being able to indulge in restaurants. I was rarely triggered to do any emotional eating and quickly identified triggers when they did occur. There has been a rather large tussle within my mind, and I can only warn you that your journey may not be easy. I have needed the support of loving friends, as well as other professionals as I have made this journey.

A year after the journey began, my weight stabilised with a thirty-kilogram (sixty-six pound) weight loss, and all blood tests showed healthy results.

Working It Through

If you still comfort-eat after disconnecting yourself from comfort food, or are still extraordinarily focused on dieting, you have not uncovered your real core belief and how it is triggered.

Uncover Core Negative Belief

Choose a period: a day, week, or month.

Choose a means to record your observations: in a notebook, on a computer or tablet, or on your phone. Write down when you

- eat between meals;
- overeat at mealtimes;
- eat seconds;
- berate yourself about being overweight;
- don't eat properly;
- eat rubbish;
- eat secretly, when no one else sees you;

- feel like you have no self-control;
- ask, "What's the point? I'll never lose weight"; or
- exercise and wonder why you bother.

Record

- what was happening;
- who did what;
- what you were saying to yourself; and
- (most importantly) what sensations you were experiencing in your body.

Float Back

Float back from those body sensations to earlier times when you experienced them.

What sensations do you experience in your body as you think of a food you have identified as a problem? Take the time to be in touch with those sensations. Write them down in a notebook or on a device.

Focus on other earlier times you experienced these physical sensations. Imagine going back through the years while focusing on what you are noticing in your body. In this way, they will connect you with memories that will help you identify your negative core belief. You don't need to force it. Just notice.

Now identify the beliefs attached to each pleasurable food. To drill down into the core belief, ask yourself: "What does this say about me as a person?" If that doesn't clarify the core belief, sometimes asking what you would think about another person displaying those traits can be of assistance.

When you think of your childhood, what belief about yourself underlies your emotional eating?

Find your core negative belief. From the following beliefs, some may resonate with you: inadequate, defective, unworthy, dirty, invisible, unlovable, don't deserve to exist, powerless, incapable, helpless, weak. There are many others. Look for those signals to follow.

Afterward, go back to desensitize yourself on any of the memories that remain disturbing. Use progressive relaxation from chapter 1, or EMDR therapy, journaling, or meditation. A friend may be all you need. Seek professional help if it continues to elude you.

Record Your Dreams

Notice what your dreams are telling you.

If you don't remember your dreams, as you go to sleep, program yourself to remember your dreams tonight. Have a pen and paper next to the bed. One way is to drink half a glass of water before going to sleep and planning to drink the other half upon waking with the intention of remembering your dreams. Tell yourself that as soon as you wake, you will write it down. Setting this intention to record your dreams is a way to programme the mind to dream and remember.

Physical Sensations

Having explored your negative belief, it is time to notice the physical sensations in your body. This is how you can tell a feeling, thought, or picture resonates within you.

Were there times you did not experience emotional eating? It is important to look for when you are not triggered, as these times can assist you to identify the positive circumstances you require.

Companions on the Journey

You might not like what you find. You are not happy. The journey may not be simple either. We are complicated creatures. I have found the journey extraordinarily difficult, far more so than I could have ever predicted. My emotional eating protected me from knowledge that would shake my very core and reorder my life. I have needed people who sincerely care for me around me to make this journey. If you are feeling some trepidation at reading these words, I suggest you look for companions. I am not suggesting you don't make the journey.

Write down the people you think will be able to support you. Write down those who might not.

Your companions for this journey may not be those around you now, for your family and friends may be quite comfortable with the way the system of your relationships are working and will not necessarily want change. If change affects your relationship as it did mine with Dan, your children may not be able to accept the new you as they have been inside the relationship and subjected to its effects, which have normalised the situation for them. They may not be ready to change.

As you change, it may force changes upon them they are neither prepared for nor willing to embrace, and they may react extremely negatively. Any system is subject to change when a component changes. My family system collapsed when I no longer fulfilled the roles assigned to me. It required more time to reform than I imagined.

Other Types of Behavioural Addictions

Maybe you don't have a weight problem related to comfort eating that addressing will help you uncover the issues of which you are vaguely aware. Bulimia, purging, gambling, drinking, retail therapy, Internet porn, or another addictive behaviour, even nail biting, can be dealt with in a similar manner as with comfort eating. Use the same techniques as illustrated with emotional eating, only replacing the concept of overeating with your addictive behaviour. Remember: seeking professional assistance is a mature response in problem solving.

Chapter 4
BREATHE, BREE; BREATHE!

Life flows with the breath
Halts in pain,
In distress.
From my journal April 2014

Horses are huge! Nearly sixty years old, and I had taken it into my head to learn how to ride! My clients are often challenged to face their fears and deal with their anxiety, and it seemed unfair to expect them to do it without doing it myself.

"Breathe, Bree; breathe," she said. My instructor commented that I was beginning to relax as she noted my knuckles were no longer white while I was gripping the reins, and I had begun to breathe during the hour I was riding.

An incident in Egypt in 2003 had seen me alone on a horse being led by a man who called himself Ali Baba. Halting amongst the rocks at the back of the great pyramids on the outskirts of Cairo, I was thankful he only wanted some extra cash. I resolved if I was going to undertake such extra travel options again to at least learn how to hold the reins myself. This did see me careening down the Andes the following year with some confidence, grasping the reins and maintaining enough control not to be thrown off Storm's back.

I woke up early this morning feeling breathless. I would have reached for the Ventolin until recently but instead slowed my breathing, recognising the anxiety. My peak flow reading is improving and is greater than the level set by my doctor[5] as a minimum for medication.

I ceased using any medications some years ago after doing the Buteyko breathing exercises. I came across information about the Buteyko method, but the cost of attending a course run by a physiotherapist seemed prohibitive. Nevertheless, the exercises were available. Besides, Daniel, a lifelong asthmatic, was very cynical about it. He has always said, "Your asthma[6] is not real asthma," perhaps recognising something that the medical profession hadn't, it being anxiety induced?

Dr. Buteyko based his method on the belief that people were over-breathing. I observed that Daniel sometimes breathed very quickly and that over the years my breathing had seemingly synchronized with his at night. I found breathing slowly to relax sometimes quite difficult.

I tested my breathing and found I could tolerate only a few seconds between exhaling and inhaling, whereas Dr. Buteyko

---

5 Do not ignore your health provider's advice, but I suggest you consider the history of your asthma from a new perspective that you can discuss with your doctor.

6 Asthma is a chronic inflammatory disease of the airways. There are many causes. A trigger causes the airways to become inflamed, narrow, and fill with mucus. It is more difficult to breathe and you cough and wheeze. One of the recognised causes of asthma is strong emotion or stress. However, I have never had any doctor talk to me about the relationship of stress or strong emotion to an asthma attack, despite my often relating to them the circumstances of an asthma attack. Nor has there ever been any recognition that asthma may be a learned behaviour, having been classically conditioned to a situation that is amenable to relearning, desensitization, or psychological therapy.

postulated that healthy people could tolerate forty to sixty seconds. During various conversations, I found people who played sports would breathe out when they got puffed, not struggle to breathe in as I did. I undertook the exercises and taught them to my child, and we were healthy and did not need asthma medication.

Time passed. Married with kids, mid-forties, unable to breathe, my doctor again diagnosed asthma and eventually persuaded me to take Pulmicort, then Symbicort. Have you ever read all the possible side effects? I certainly had sore throats, coughs, and respiratory infections, problems with vision, and weight gain, to mention a few. No one ever suggested they were possibly side effects of my medications.

I had succumbed to the belief that I was growing old and that was the reason for my breathlessness. I no longer believed I could manage to breathe easily without medication because my lungs were old. COPD (chronic obstructive pulmonary disease) was predicted to be my fate when, in my fifties after a respiratory test, I was informed I had the lungs of an eighty-year-old and that matters would only worsen if I did not manage my asthma appropriately with preventive medications.

Obesity and reflux, with gastro-oesophageal reflux disease (GORD) a possible culprit, were also involved. Latterly I experienced heartburn, but possibly my frequent experiences of sore throat related to reflux too.

Investigating treatment for bronchitis, I found mention of pulmonary rehabilitation programs. No one ever suggested as an adult that I undertake such a programme, despite being told many years ago I would develop COPD. I have always believed I had weak lungs. The medical advice was directed at obtaining my compliance with taking asthma preventers. The risk of chronic bronchitis also increases for those non-smokers who are regularly exposed to smoke, such as those who live with a smoker. My father never gave up smoking, and cigarette ashtrays were in abundance around the house.

I found breathing through a straw for a couple of minutes and becoming aware of the panic was a means of desensitizing myself too. However, there were many triggers and events connected with my anxiety-induced asthma that required a more systematic approach.

Subsequent to what I now recognise as a very emotional occasion of a family wedding, I fell into a heap, so to speak, and had been using preventive medications again for more than a year. I had not been paying any attention to my breathing with regard to the exercises I had once practised nor to my need for managing anxiety through slow gentle breathing, relaxation, or other stress-management techniques.

While I always thought I was a lonely child, always well behaved and staying in the house as I was told, I had begun to think I was depressed and came to the conclusion that I was very anxious. Rather than being good and obedient, I began to think I was a scared little rabbit that never left the burrow. It was time to process the anxiety that induced my asthma.

Float Back to Identify Touchstone Memory

Once again I focused on the problem and let come to mind what would. Closing my eyes, I imagined floating back through the years, while concentrating on the physical sensations. In this case, the physical sensations were of being unable to breath easily. My chest and shoulders were tight. There was tension in my throat.

This was quite scary, and I worried it might trigger an asthma attack, so I was cautious. Every time I experienced an asthma attack, I formed a memory of that attack. These memories are all connected. They are layered. The kernel was the present symptom, with the layers of memory possibly increasing the severity of symptoms through activating memories, contributing to strong emotional responses that might worsen the symptoms. I kept reminding myself I was revisiting a memory, so any sense of not being able to breathe I interpreted as part of a memory.

Having experienced breathlessness, I let my mind notice events throughout my life span of when I had problems with breathing. Although I knew the float-back technique can take some time (I started with the present and then allowed the bodily sensations to take me back down the years, one decade at a time), I found my thoughts immediately focused on the first time I had a problem. As I had practised bridging the present sensations with the past, I trained my brain in the process, and it sought what was needed with greater ease.

I had chicken pox during first grade. As my mother said, I was always healthy until I started school, so suffering measles must have been when I was in kindergarten, and I developed bronchial pneumonia as a complication. I don't remember the pneumonia. I remember doing breathing exercises morning and night, pumping my arms up and down ten times or until it made me cough to rid myself of the "gunk" in my chest. Dad was a heavy smoker, and he seemed to do this coughing without any arm-pumping action required! It was not a lovely way to start the day.

The Touchstone Event

Looking at that exercise that marked me apart from other children, certainly as unhealthy compared to my sister, I realised my negative cognition or belief about myself was that "I am sickly." Then it morphed into "I am defective, like an old man; like my father." Of course, you must forgive me for that child's viewpoint (he was only twenty-eight!). What would I rather think about myself when I see that image of me doing my exercises? The positive cognition I would prefer would be that "I am getting better." How true did that feel? My VoC (validity of cognition) was three out of seven, not quite halfway to believing it. I was worried and anxious, and the sensations of those emotions I felt, unsurprisingly, in my chest, but also in my stomach. My SUDS (subjective units of distress scale) was four out of ten, where zero is a neutral or calm state and ten is as disturbed as one could possibly feel.

I decided to use bilateral stimulation by tapping the outer sides of my thighs. This was an unusual choice for me. The butterfly hug,[7] with my arms wrapped across my chest to touch the upper arm, seemed to further constrict my breathing, and I didn't want to use eye movements. I trusted my instinct as to what was most appropriate. Although I believe there are many natural ways we use bilateral stimulation, I was cautious about using self-directed EMDR therapy. I took it slowly to see how I responded and knew I could seek professional help if the emotions and bodily sensations became extremely powerful, as they very well might have.

I recorded what I noticed after each set of thirty-second duration of alternate thigh tapping. There was a band of tightness across my chest and tension in my throat. I saw a little girl, her dark hair pulled back on one side with a bow, with very skinny little arms going up and down, until she coughed.

Tapping the sides of my thighs, my SUDS went down to two and then one as the tension eased in my throat. The band across my chest relaxed. My SUDS became zero. It occurred to me how frequently I have had sore throats throughout my life, always thinking I had a virus or bacteria.

I yawned, a common occurrence when doing EMDR processing. My positive cognition changed to "I am healthy," with a VoC (validity of cognition) of four, where one meant I did not believe it in relation to this memory and seven meant I believed it completely. I continued tapping, this time on my knees, picturing the image of

---

7 The butterfly hug describes crossing your arms across your chest, placing your middle finger under the collarbone, spreading out your other fingers, linking your thumbs to form the body of the butterfly, and then alternating lifting each hand as the wings of the butterfly:
http://www.emdrtherapyvolusia.com/downloads/lynda_documents/forms_protocols_and_scripts/The_Butterfly_Hug_Protocol_April_2011.pdf.

that little girl, who was looking in the mirror, smiling, and thinking, *I am healthy.*

I then closed my eyes and brought up my target memory, though the image had changed. No longer did I see a little girl, pumping her arms up and down, but the reflection of myself smiling in the mirror. I knew from experience with my clients and myself that the image sometimes simply fades, becomes distant, or is replaced with a different scene.

Closing my eyes to allow myself to focus on the memory, I said to myself, "I am healthy." I scanned my body to see if there was any residual sensation left, and I began to burp twenty or thirty times. My belief had changed to "My body knows how to heal."

To ensure the connection between the now-processed memory and the positive belief, I imagined bringing them together and tapped on my knees for about thirty seconds. I again closed my eyes, focusing on the memory, simultaneously thinking, *My body knows how to heal,* until there were no disturbing sensations in my body.

The next day I checked my SUDS level. It remained at zero. It was important to recheck the SUDS rating, as it is not unusual for it to increase, as further-connected material is accessed and would have needed processing. In EMDR therapy, this earliest memory is known as the touchstone event, meaning the first event that occurred where the relevant life disturbance took place. Too often people believe that to be significant, an event needs to be life threatening in a medically traumatic manner. Having discovered with so many clients, as well as myself, the events that often shape our lives have been overlooked because they seem so ordinary.

Reviewing this many months later, I noted a distance in my connection with it. I could be reading about any little girl. It no longer has any emotional impact on me, confirming that this had been successfully processed.

Processing Further Memories

Processing one memory, in this case my first memory connected with difficulty with breathing, was insufficient to eradicate the problem. I knew there had to be other potent memories.

At age eleven, I was diagnosed with an asthma attack. I was breathless after dancing a lot with my older cousin at his sister's wedding in 1958. There was a lot of smoke in the air, as all the guys smoked in that era, and some of the women too. I can see my dad stumbling, angry—there is something going on: some fighting, arguing, and Mum saying something about mixing beer and whiskey. Anyway, I can't breathe. It is the next day, I imagine, when the doctor said I had asthma, but I don't remember any treatment.

Once again I used alternate thigh tapping to target the memory. I could have used eye movements. "I am sickly" stills seemed to fit, though there was a resonance with "I am defective." The emotions were fear and annoyance, and the SUDS was four, with a pain across my back and tightness in my chest. Now I noted I would prefer the positive belief of "I am healthy." My validity of cognition (VoC) is midrange, meaning I halfway believed the statement "I am healthy."

My thoughts turned to the fact that people should not be smoking, and I needed some fresh air. I don't understand why people want to get drunk at weddings and not remember a lovely occasion. I processed this to a zero with no unpleasant body sensations remaining, or a clear body-scan, to be technical.

Reviewing this later, I noted there was a resonance with a negative belief of "I am not in control." This may be a possible target for future work, but the image no longer holds any emotional charge for me.

Other Memories

A third memory surfaced. The image was of the church during a student's funeral, her siblings at the lectern. Continuing processing, using eye movements, I targeted this. After each set of eye movements, I noted each new memory that came. Years later, an uncle dying from lung cancer, unable to catch his breath, and then a death from anaphylaxis, and my own choking episodes are all processed. "She has a small swallow," echoed in my mother's voice, "just like me." Sometimes the connection between memories was not immediately obvious.

Yet another memory rose of my walking from the kitchen into the playroom and picking up my toddler and tipping him upside down. I had no prior conscious understanding of what I was doing or why, and put him over my knee. I pounded a couple of times on his back until he coughed up a coin. This memory still amazes me. How did I know?

When talking to my auntie Agatha during my father's fiftieth birthday party, I discovered she was seeing a doctor the following week with worries about her asthma. She was not quite sixty-two. Shortly afterward I noticed she was slumped down in a lounge chair. She had died. I was twenty-seven at the time. Following processing, this soon had no emotional charge for me.

Years passed and a most tragic event occurred. The son of dear friends ended his own life. I'd had no idea of his depression and felt, as a school counsellor, I should have been able to help. My assuming any responsibility was inappropriate but nevertheless happened. I believed I had badly let my friends down. I couldn't breathe. Again my doctor diagnosed asthma, and I spent a week at home recovering. Diagnosis seems to have been based on a low-peak flow, and listening to the lungs with a stethoscope. Medication was prescribed.

I did not expect processing this to be easy.

The description of his death, even though I did not see it physically, stuck in my mind. My SUDS was eight, and my negative cognition was "I am useless," which is but a variant of my default position of "I am not good enough." The contrasting positive cognition (or belief) I preferred to be attached to this memory of "I can help" had a validity of cognition (VoC) of two out of seven. Again understandably, the experience of anxiety and sadness was tightness in my chest.

I hadn't even realised I was still distressed about this until it emerged as a memory connected with my targeting my asthma. Though rationally I know it had nothing to do with not being good enough, the emotional reaction centres on that core belief. The image is replaced by one of his mother at lunch recently, letting me know how worthwhile she feels I am. I am so grateful for her continuing love.

Then the memory that surfaced was when one of my children was diagnosed with asthma. The image was one of the preschool staff refusing attendance, because of the coughing. I was holding my four-year-old and saying, "Let's go; they don't want us here." Talk about not feeling good enough!

Again the negative cognition was "I am not good enough."

The positive cognition was "I am worthy," with the meaning of "I can be trusted" and "I am telling you it is asthma, not a virus or flu, and I wouldn't bring anyone if they were infectious." The VoC measured five out of seven, so it felt nearly true when I thought of this scene.

I focused on my body. The tension was in my arms as I held my child, in my chest and face, feeling humiliated and angry at the preschool teacher's rejection. My SUDS was four out of ten, rapidly processed with thigh tapping.

Immediately, images of assertive people in my life arose, and I heard, "I can be assertive": "Don't be ridiculous; I wouldn't bring anyone if they were ill and infectious. I've given the asthma medication. We've been to the doctor to assess if there was any infectiousness, and I'm offended you have spoken to me this way." Wow, did that feel good!

I realised that whenever there was illness, I felt disempowered. The SUDS stayed stuck at one. Asking myself why, I recognised it was because I needed to talk to my now grown child. If I processed it anymore, my brain felt it would forget. I had no idea my brain had feelings!

I finished the processing, so the SUDS went down to zero, and my body was relaxed.

Titrating a Memory

It was time to deal with the most recent experience of developing asthma after a wedding. Though it was lovely to see them happy, there were a lot of emotions surrounding their wedding.

I had a very bad reflux condition, and I believe I experienced reflux-induced asthma after the wedding reception. Too much food and champagne, I imagined! Asthma medication did not work, though I had been persuaded to use preventive medication. After an emergency visit to the doctor, I was given medication that was so powerful, if I took it for longer than three days, I was warned I would have to taper off using a careful procedure of reducing the dose.

If I had worked with an EMDR therapist on this problem of asthma, I most likely would have targeted the first memory of my breathing exercises and then this one, which I judged as the worst. However, my mind had decided to follow a timeline, and I have trusted my instincts, as the brain knows how to heal if given the chance.

I was afraid of accessing the whole memory, as it may have been too distressing. I chose one small aspect of it so I was not flooded with emotions and unable to continue. It was especially important, as I did not want to trigger an asthma attack. I did not want to be re-traumatised if I accessed the memory and then left it unprocessed because it was too emotionally charged to continue. Brain studies show that I had a five-hour window when I revisited a traumatic memory in which I could rework it so it was no longer distressing, but I was not sure it was enough time to ring up a psychologist for an emergency appointment!

The image of this time was my sitting at the reception, across the table from another couple and a pre-schooler. By nine o'clock, Daniel took home his elderly uncle, as he was tired. Dan did not return. Hours later, I arrived home to find them chatting away in the living room. I daresay from Dan's point of view he had done the noble thing of keeping his uncle company and it might be seen as selfish on my part that I wanted him to return to be with me.

Once again the negative cognition was "I am not good enough," having morphed from "I am not important enough for Dan to return to the reception to be with me or to drive me home."

The positive cognition was "I am worthy," with the concomitant meaning of "I am important." The VoC measured six out of seven, so it felt nearly true when I thought of this scene.

Again, burping, tightness in chest, dismay, disbelief that I am left there in this situation, alone. My SUDS was eight out of ten.

I was not sure I could process this on my own with thigh tapping. I thought I might have to take a little of the scene, or a little bit of the feeling rather than the whole memory, lest I be overwhelmed.

There was a pain in my back, on my left lung. I remembered I had pleurisy when I was eighteen.

Processing Continues for the Next Twenty-Four to Forty-Eight Hours

The next morning I woke at four thirty. I had not shut down the memory, and my brain had continued processing. I had thought I had not activated it enough, but the experience of "reflux" ten-and-a-half hours after eating a small meal called that into question. It did not make sense that after six months I should again experience the heartburn, indigestion, and discomfort that had been diagnosed as reflux. However, it made perfect sense that it was part of the memory of the wedding.

Once again the body remembered. The symptoms were not age-related but part of a memory.

I did some slow, gentle, abdominal breathing. Although I have taught people for nearly thirty years to place their right hand on their tummy and their left on their chest, as they imagine a balloon in their tummy that gently inflates and deflates, for some unknown reason I reversed the positions of my hands. The pain gradually decreased, confirming that it was indeed part of a memory, not a physical symptom of a present problem.

In the dawning light I added eye movements, scanning across the top of the closet doors. Gradually the SUDS reduced from a seven to a four. I added the light pressure of my hands to the heart centre, where I was experiencing the pain, noticing that my left hand was numb, the little finger and ring finger more so. Then the SUDS eventually dropped to a 0.5. I asked myself why it wouldn't go any lower and realised I wanted to be able to remember the experience the next morning.

The reading on my peak flow meter (which measures how well air comes out of the lungs after inhaling fully) at nine o'clock in the morning was quite low, 200 compared with my usual 300. A few breaths brought it back to 260, but it took a few more anxiety-reducing breaths to bring it back to 300, as it was by nine twenty. This again confirmed the brain had chosen the physical symptoms and worked on them while I was asleep. This made perfect sense as the previous evening I had decided it would be too big a memory for me to process on my own, bringing up all the images, the body sensations, the emotions, and the beliefs. I had told my brain it needed to titrate the experience, selecting a small part of it, so it went ahead and did that, as it is meant to do, processing the memory while I was asleep, until the disturbance woke me.

Having desensitized one channel of the memory, that of the physical sensations, I next chose the image of the table at the reception by focusing on the little child. As soon as I did, I realised I had played with her because I didn't want her to feel lonely or unimportant. I ran around the dance floor, playing hide and seek with her. With alternating thigh tapping, the SUDS subsided quickly from a six to a two. I knew she was not lonely and was enjoying the wedding. Then I broadened the image to include the pre-schooler's grandmother.

The SUDS rose to three or four. I couldn't really talk with her as the band was noisy and I was across the other side of the large round table. I felt quite alone. The negative cognition was "I am not important." My chest was tingling, anxious. I used the butterfly hug,[iii] with my thumbs interlaced, tapping my hands, fingers spread, alternately on my upper chest. *I can cope. I am okay. Everyone is fine. Everything is okay.*

It became hard to see any image. It wasn't as noisy, and my body felt more relaxed. There was a little tightness in my throat. The image in my head was that I went home and told Dan I felt lonely when he didn't come back. Shoulder tapping continued, but the feelings didn't subside, so I switched to horizontal eye movements. No one was there for me, but I could handle it. I began to burp.

I focused on the whole scene: the feelings, the body sensations, and the thoughts. I placed my hands over the centre of my chest. It was okay. I imagined I saw their baby, born the next year. *They are happy. I am okay. I am worthy.*

Did this mean I would never feel breathless again? No, but it did show me that by addressing the emotional issues connected with my "asthma," I could control those asthmatic symptoms quite successfully. Hours later, my peak flow remained at a healthy reading of 300.

At the time of the event, I was not thinking these things about myself. That is, I was not consciously thinking, *I am not important.* It was as though my brain filed experiences under categories, and when I processed them through using EMDR therapy, journaling, meditation, or counselling, the neural network led me from one event to the next. This led to healing of this memory so it no longer held the strong negative charge of emotions when I thought about it, and so it no longer affected me.

*

That afternoon I had scheduled a therapy session with my psychologist. It was after I had separated from Dan. Earlier, at lunch my girlfriend had disclosed a comment she said was made several years ago. On seeing an older man with a young Filipina, Dan reportedly had asked why he couldn't have one like that. It was probably a joke but it stuck in my mind, and I felt quite angry, and when my therapist asked how I was feeling, I decided I needed to process the anger. Whether or not it happened was not the point. It was a catalyst that triggered awareness of the anger that I was holding in my body.

As Dr. Shapiro, the developer of EMDR therapy, reiterates frequently, "The past is present." I found that the recent wedding again featured in what I needed to process, but going from the feeling of anger, it opened a whole different set of memories. This of course demonstrated the benefit I was able to gain from working with a skilled therapist rather than doing a self-directed session.

Unexpectedly, the anger initially focussed on Dan's car that was quite spacious in the back. Many family brides had accepted the offer of being driven to their weddings in it. Other people generally are not allowed to drive it, and in any case, the likely drivers, being my sons, were often busy with roles in the wedding party. This resulted in my having to find my own way to a lot of weddings. As a result there was often the problem of two cars at the reception as well, so I also drove myself home.

Whether I was distressed or excited, joyful or sad, I was on my own much of the time. The newly married couples usually asked to be driven to a distant photo-opportunity picturesque spot, and

I remained to entertain guests between ceremony and reception. I felt I was always alone.

My SUDS was nine out of a possible ten when we began, but my therapist skilfully guided my brain and body to a relaxed zero.

Always the decision was based on practicality, but it had unintentionally wounded me, a wound that I thought was healed but festered, out of my conscious awareness, as I ate myself into ill health, as I sat on the edge of my life. It is easy to see the connection between the childhood fear of abandonment and triggering of those fears at a subconscious level in these episodes. Talking sense to myself did not make the bodily sensations go away. I needed to process the memory not ignore it or create an alternative.

Not being able to breathe was scary for me as a child. I probably accepted restrictions on swimming underwater because I was afraid of not being able to breathe. I found sports hard for the same reason. I would joyfully greet signs of my menstrual period as an excuse to miss PE. Pity I was such a late starter.

Several months later I was monitoring my breathing regularly, for it had been an emotionally charged time. I found I could hold my breath longer without discomfort, but it was still only for twenty-one seconds, and I knew I needed to improve this. Mid-2013 I separated[8] from Dan. I was unwell. I had asthmatic symptoms. I felt as if I was choking. Momentarily I wondered if I had a chest infection. However, I knew how to successfully deal with the anxiety so I could deal with the breathlessness, so I focused on slowing my breathing and recognised what my emotions were telling me. I asked for support from my friends and found it.

November 2013: "This morning I woke feeling nauseated. It was the first time I was expecting my friends to visit me since my separation. I went to the shops to buy fresh vegetables and returned home to begin preparation for lunch, hoping the nausea would pass. However, it didn't, and I soon found myself over the toilet

[8] The second half of the book explains this more in depth.

bowl, vomiting. This was uncomfortable to say the least, given I had not been able to have breakfast. I thought perhaps the fish or pesto last night was to blame, but as the former was frozen and the latter not passed the use-by date, that didn't seem an adequate explanation."

However, by the time my friends arrived, I was feeling sufficiently capable of cooking and conversing, being an expert at ignoring my feelings to focus on others.

After they left, clearing away and cleaning up having been accomplished (no slacking off here), I lay down for a few hours. Upon waking, I realised these feelings were familiar. My brain had obviously done its own float back. The earliest discomfort that came to mind was my girlfriend's wedding day I mentioned before. Two days earlier I had been told there was no future in the relationship. As her maid of honour, I could not tell her of my heartbreak, made poignant when she declared it would be my time (to marry) soon.

I realised with a shock how much I had believed my girlfriend had an emotional investment in my relationship. Subsequently, after I had gone away to the country to teach, and Daniel proposed to me weeks later, she featured frequently in his letters endorsing our marriage, excited for both of us being married. When I lunched with her in mid 2013, to discuss how very unhappy I was, I knew in all likelihood the dream of us celebrating our golden wedding anniversaries was about to be destroyed.

Processing this memory of her wedding later with my psychologist, my negative cognition was "I am a bad person" for having lied. This soon became "I am not good enough," because if I was, I would be worthy of being married like her. My positive cognition could have been "I am good enough," but instead it was "I have the right to express my feelings."

My emotions included anxiety and a fear of rejection. They were felt physically all down the centre of my torso from my throat to my stomach. My SUDS was seven.

During processing, I became aware of the connection between my anxiety and my frequent sore throats. Often a doctor reluctantly gave me antibiotics, although they could not see any redness. A dry throat is a common symptom of anxiety.

Also, the early memory of when they were married, and we were not, but had arranged to have a dinner party at my parents' home surfaced. I cooked meatballs in wine sauce as an entrée and managed to allow the oil to burst into flame and burn my mother's kitchen curtains.

Neither interested in eating nibbles before my guests' arrival nor a whiskey, which once was a treat, I found myself confronted with the raw emotions of shame and anxiety unrelieved by emotional eating. My friends had no idea how I felt over the years. Not surprising, as I had not fully comprehended my feelings either. I used emotional eating to deal with my emotions before I was consciously aware of them.

Other episodes came up as I continued to process the memories using EMDR therapy. Gradually, I had learned to be a good cook and stopped worrying that my children and home were inferior, and then I could enjoy their company. However, any perceived slight was magnified by my anxiety and over the years required some stern talking sense to myself. It is such a relief to realise I can let this all go and can now enjoy their company in the way I did as a teenager.

Returning to the target memory of my friend's wedding day, I found the image was blurry and my SUDS score was down to two out of ten.

It had been agreed that the year we all turned seventy-five, there was to be a very special celebration. I had not realised how this impacted me until that day, in that I believed I let everyone down. There was no way all four of us were ever going to be in the same room again in order to celebrate anything together. They, however, do not hold this against me at all. Again measuring the SUDS, it was down to 1.5, and the image was very faded. Although the SUDS decreased to 0.5 with further processing, it wasn't until I mentioned to my psychologist that I had trouble with the positive cognition that I made a quick completion of processing the target.

She commented that "I have the right to express my feelings" was "piss weak," and she asked what did it say about me as a person! Yes, I am worthwhile! This is so much more satisfactory. It took several sets of eye movements installing the positive belief for me to remain comfortable in my body when I thought about the memory and the belief. It was very pleasant to have a relaxed throat at last.

Oesophageal Spasm

February 2014: oesophageal spasm sounds a bit frightening. I did not know what this was until the previous November when a doctor colleague, after witnessing an attack, explained it to me. Until then I assumed for some reason I was choking and could not catch my breath. I had already noticed it was related to anxiety and could occur if I was eating or drinking. The occasion was my presenting the information I had learned about emotional eating to fifty or sixty EMDR clinicians. A little anxiety was present there!

The spasms are painful muscle contractions that affect the hollow tube between your throat and your stomach. They feel like sudden, severe chest pain and may last a few minutes or much longer, but they occurred infrequently. More frequent spasms can prevent food and liquids from travelling through the oesophagus. The spasms can lead to chronic pain and swallowing problems.

I did not recognise that I needed to do some processing on it until in the realtor's office I experienced an attack that was somewhat humiliating. Eating or drinking very hot or very cold foods or drinks, heartburn, gastro-oesophageal reflux disease (GORD), and anxiety are all viewed as risk factors. Certainly I had experienced choking when I also had reflux, but the endoscopy showed no abnormalities. It seemed X-rays may be ordered, along with other tests to monitor

PH to see if stomach acid was flowing back up the oesophagus, and the strength of the muscle contracting can also be measured. I thought attempting some self-directed EMDR therapy wouldn't hurt prior to visiting the family doctor.

I identified the most distressing memory I had of the experience. Perhaps eight years ago, while in the kitchen, I remember being doubled over unable to breathe, choking. I was not aware of anyone else around despite the fact that it occurred on a Sunday evening when all my family and grandchildren would have been present. Memories that are emotionally charged are like that. They appear to be very vivid but don't contain everything that actually occurred.

The negative cognition was "I don't deserve to be looked after."

My positive cognition was "I do deserve to be looked after."

However, my level of belief in this was only a three. That is, on the VoC scale, where one is untrue and seven completely true, I could not even half-believe I deserved to be cared for.

My SUDS was seven, my throat, unsurprisingly, was constricted, and I felt anxious, the same as I did in the realtor's office the previous day.

Using horizontal eye movements, I noted the memories that were connected. Approximately every twenty seconds I noted what new material came to mind. Beginning with the present, I thought I would not deserve to be looked after when I grew older. After twenty seconds of eye movements, I experienced intense pain in my bowel and throat, and felt fluid gathering in my throat, but it was not the sensation of saliva, and it made me think of blood and when I had haemorrhaged as a seven-and-a-half-year-old after a tonsillectomy. I had been very messy, vomiting all over my bed, and was sent to hospital alone in the ambulance. Accompanying me in the ambulance would not have occurred to my mother, thinking it was not permitted, or perhaps she was terrified.

Twenty seconds later, and I remembered my mother clinging to the doorpost as she was being carried on a stretcher, being taken by ambulance to hospital, pleading that I not let them take her. She'd had a heart attack and needed to go to emergency. As a seven-year-old, she had probably seen her mother taken by ambulance to hospital and had not seen her again before she died.

Referring back to my target memory, I saw myself doubled over, believing "no one can help me; I am on my own." With each set of bilateral simulation using eye movements, I asked myself, what am I noticing now? Then I noted pain in my knee and saw myself collapsed on the sidewalk, after Dan had said our relationship was finished.

The next memory was some twenty years ago, when I fell off a ladder and hit my head. Dan told me I was fine, but I insisted on an ambulance being called. The paramedics were kind and considerate and reassured me after checking me properly. No one stayed with me while I waited for the ambulance, though my children and their friends came up to see me lying there.

Another set of eye movements, again lasting about thirty seconds, and there was a new memory connected with my target memory. When I had chest pains a couple of years ago, without private health insurance (as it was too expensive) I refused to go on a public hospital waiting list for possibly twelve months before I could undertake the stress test for my heart, so I paid for the stress test myself. I was not going to wait, as this did not seem like taking care of myself very well at all.

I started feeling very sleepy while processing. When in labour with my fifth child, I felt my need to be looked after was ignored. Dan's injuries from his recent car accident (see chapter 6) inspired greater concern, as he was sent home. I am sure this was a sensible decision on the part of the nursing staff but it left me unsupported. Drowsiness was part of the memory I was processing.

After some more bilateral stimulation, additional memories or thoughts surfaced: "If things are hard, I have to do it on my own." "I can but I don't want to." Another set of eye movements, and I remembered I enjoyed travelling to Hobart on my own, writing my book, working. I felt competent. "Even though I am strong and resilient, I want to feel looked after. I deserve to be looked after."

Checking in with how my body was feeling, I found my SUDS was reduced to 1.5.

Checking the target memory, the image had changed. I was sitting up, and I was okay. I was relieved. I saw there were professionals present that could look after me. It was okay to be looked after. "It is okay to ask for help."

SUDS was reduced to one.

I thought, *My feelings deserve to be respected. If I am afraid, I don't deserve to be mocked or told there is nothing wrong. I deserve to be comforted. I deserve to be held when I am afraid. It is okay to be afraid. It is okay to be strong too. All my feelings are okay. It is okay to express my feelings. I deserve to ask for my needs to be met.*

Checking the target memory, I saw I was walking away, saying good-bye to the paramedics and I was okay.

SUDS was reduced to 0.5.

I asked myself what was stopping the SUDS going to zero. Questioning myself this way opened up a new set of memories that I processed.

As I didn't expect to be looked after, I made a flippant remark that sounded like I did not need to be cared for, that there was no problem. My feelings were not congruent with my words.

The next memory that arose was when I was pregnant with my first child, and we only had a three-quarter-sized bed. It was narrower than a double bed. *Aren't I lucky I have a bed?* Eleanor Porter's *Pollyanna* was alive and well inside my mind, always looking on the bright side. I practised positive psychology long before it became trendy. I was uncomfortable and often afraid I would fall out, but there was not enough money to buy a bed. As well, we were staying in a relative's spare room.

After giving birth, when I came home with my week-old son from hospital, I felt rewarded when there was a new queen-size bed. I don't know how money became available, and I guess I was too busy to ask. We did not have a washing machine. I washed nappies (diapers) by hand. This was before the era of disposable nappies. I had asked for a washing machine in my letters before we were married. My needs did not feel like they were important.

I checked my SUDS on the original target memory. It was now zero. My VoC was seven out of seven. I now believed completely that "I deserve to be looked after." My body remained relaxed when I thought about it.

The insight I gained from this was that I had dealt with anxiety throughout my life and that I chose a partner who wasn't anxious, who knew what he wanted, and who set about getting it.

Working It Through

Write down any physical symptom you experience, whether or not it is a regular occurrence. Write down any aches, pains, or upsets in any part of your body. Focusing on that physical experience, float back through the years to other times that pain or part of your body or experience occurred. Think of the history of that part of your body.

Early life disturbances[9] impact people throughout their lives. Children who experience trauma early in their life are much more likely to suffer PTSD and other mental-health problems in their adulthood than those who did not experience trauma. They might

---

[9] See http://www.cdc.gov/violenceprevention/acestudy/for details on the adverse childhood experiences (ACE) study. The total amount of stress during childhood is measured under headings of emotional, physical, and sexual abuse, emotional and physical neglect, and household dysfunction including domestic violence, substance abuse including alcohol, mental illness, separation, divorce, and imprisonment of a parent. As the number of adverse childhood experiences increase, the risk for adult health problems increases multifold.

See also Vincent J. Felitti MD, FACP, et al. "Relationship of Childhood Abuse and Household Dysfunction to Many of the Leading Causes of Death in Adults"; the Adverse Childhood Experiences *(*ACE*)* Study, *American Journal of Preventive Medicine*, Volume 14, Issue 4, 245–58, May 1998. Retrieved from http://www.ajpmonline.org/article/S0749-3797(98)00017-8/abstract.

not have an episodic memory of a particular traumatic event, but their body remembers.

Affect Bridge

To identify the emotions attached to those physical symptoms, begin by closing your eyes, bringing to mind the occasion, focusing on the physical sensations, and allowing your body to carry your mind back to other occasions you experienced these same physical sensations and emotions. This is similar to the float-back technique described at the end of the previous chapter. Here the emphasis is on the emotions rather than the physical sensations.

Desensitize with EMDR therapy, progressive relaxation, journaling, or meditation.

Chapter 5

CHILDHOOD

The truth will set you free.
—John 8:32, English Standard Version

Tinker, tailor, soldier, sailor,
Whom do I like best,
Who is nearest to daddy dearest,
He I like the best.
—From my journal, April 5, 2013

I was under the blankets, my face covered. Perhaps it was a bit colder that morning (March 11, 2013) as autumn was here, and though the warmth builds during the day, it can begin on the chilly side. It is funny I wrote "under the blankets" as we have only used doonas[10] for decades, but it was the emotional blanket that operated as a barrier that I was remembering.

What did I sense in my body as I lay there? There was constriction in my throat. I was unable to talk, unable to say I love you, unable to hear it said to me. Certainly I couldn't see anything, as my eyes were

[10] Continental quilt, or comforter: a soft flat bag filled with wool, feathers, down or silk.

closed. There was a weight on my head, the blanket. I felt smothered. I couldn't breathe. There was a panicky feeling in my chest.

I remembered the noise of the siren screaming, as I felt buffeted by the sway of the vehicle that raced away from my home. I was alone in the ambulance. The family doctor had been called to make a home visit after I had been allowed to watch the firecrackers lit by my father in the backyard while I was well rugged up in a blanket. It was Empire Day, observed on May 24, Queen Victoria's birthday. People always bought a small amount of fireworks to celebrate. Sometimes people gathered and built bonfires but I never attended one during my childhood.

Despite being six and a half, I slept in a large cot[11] in the dining room of my aunt's house, which was where the doctor examined me, feeling where the lymph glands at the top of my leg were swollen. He said I had scarlet fever, and my mother urgently asked him if I would lose all my hair. I can see her anxious face quite clearly. I found this distressing.

After ten days with scarlet fever in a hospital isolation ward, being injected each day in my buttocks with what seemed like huge needles, and no visits from my parents, I was bathed and dressed by a nurse in preparation for going home. I can feel the trembling in my body as I stood naked being towelled dry. She was a different nurse to the one who had cut off my fingernails, telling me I was too young to have them long. It had been lonely and scary, but I was glad to be going home.

I skipped across the grass in front of the hospital to the car they had borrowed to fetch me. Daddy would have been driving, so I don't know why for a long time I thought I sat on his lap wrapped up in a blanket, unable to see him. I wanted him to love me again. I wanted to feel secure and safe. I wanted him to tell me he loved me, but he didn't. Being wrapped in a blanket wasn't what happened, it wasn't the actual event, but it felt real. It was genuine in its representation of

[11] A large crib used for infants and babies.

my emotional isolation, inability to seek communication, invisibility of self, inability to be contacted or protected and invisible to others.

Indeed, this memory was one that formed some important emotional work for me in my forties, when I was doing postgraduate studies, and to resolve it then I had phoned my father and asked him to tell me he loved me, which he did. The next time I saw him in person, he pushed aside others saying, "I need to tell my daughter something." It felt like he took me up in his arms and told me he loved me.

Well that should be it, shouldn't it? All gone, over, better. Why does another quarter of a century whizz past before a new insight? Busy were we? Who put that blanket there, and who kept it there? Ha, me? No, not possible. I surely didn't pattern all my relationships on that paradigm, did I?

Oh yes I did. It is rather distressing to note this. I have tolerated not being told I am loved. I have expected not to be told and chosen people who wouldn't tell me! If I had been told or given any compliment, I would have had little idea how to handle it.

This point in my relationship with my father was pivotal. There are things that were true about me beforehand that were very different afterward, and although the image of the blanket is but a metaphor for the emotional event, it has not only coloured my life, it has shaped it with Dan, my children, my friends, my sister and my professional colleagues and acquaintances. It set me up to expect a lack of communication and physical closeness as normal, so I accepted very little as sufficient when it wasn't. It was useful with clients as there was never any expectation from me that the relationship was mutual, which is rather a good thing for a psychologist.

Before my hospital experience, there was a warm physical closeness with my parents and little sister. Afterward, there was distance. Games of tipping us upside down and kissing us and roughhousing on the floor disappeared. I don't remember anything physically affectionate other than ritualised kissing on the mouth before we went to bed. Yet I remember my mother scoffing at people who offered their cheek to be kissed. She took that as an insult to mean she was not good enough to kiss properly on the mouth. I cannot remember hugs, nor can my sister. She would mock one of my aunts, who sat with her arms around her daughters on their rare visits.

Holding those feelings in my awareness, I brought to mind all my romantic relationships, allowing the memories to surface.

It seems silly, but the first thought is of the little five-year-old boy who chased me in kindergarten. I am laughing and happy. The goal of the game was to catch the girl and kiss her. Then I am cuddled up on a lounge with a boy. I am fourteen. Nothing said, nothing to hear. A long time between kisses. Who was the first boy who kissed me? He was the son of family friends, and I remember the warmth of the physical closeness.

Around fourteen and a half, the next boy who paid me any attention was my boyfriend for the following five years. I can remember quite clearly as he was kissing me outside the hall where the youth club met that he queried whether I would be proud with him. I remember being confused over "being proud with him," meaning to be proud I was with him or being arrogant and haughty? He really wanted to know if I was likely to slap his hand away if he touched me intimately. Evidently I wasn't. I accepted whatever was given and certainly didn't ask for more. Again, what I accepted as intimacy was only a physical closeness.

It wasn't until I mentioned months after I separated from Daniel that this first boyfriend was three years older than me, and a colleague queried me, that I realised I had been groomed for sex from the age of fourteen. Five years ago, when a client disclosed to me the sexual demands made upon her by a seventeen-year-old when she was fourteen, I was able to recognise the child sexual abuse inherent in her story and assist her. We were able to process the trauma using EMDR therapy. I had managed not to ever consider that this was similar for me.

I was still a child at fourteen and should have been protected. Instead, my parents encouraged the relationship even though the main occupation was going to drive-in movies where I rarely saw a complete movie as the windows were steamed up and we were in the backseat. My parents' only stipulation was I had to have my homework done before he visited during the week each Tuesday and Thursday.

The stated reason for permitting this relationship was that as a teenager, Mum had been forbidden to have a boyfriend until she was sixteen. It amazes me that her resentment toward her eldest sister, who had raised her from the age of seven, had misled her so badly. Rather than appreciating the care and protection she had been afforded, Mum abrogated her responsibility toward me in the name of a poorly reasoned sense of entitlement.

Thirty years later, Mum told me that she had broken off a friendship of many years when the woman had warned her that we must have been having sex. Even then, after she knew it was true, her reaction was that it was my responsibility, as after all, she hadn't had premarital sex. Despite two decades of education about the nature of child sexual abuse, she still could not recognise it. I can hardly condemn her when I didn't and indeed when our whole society could not.

At one of the school reunions I shared my carefully preserved school magazines with my classmates. We were startled to find an article I had written when I was fifteen. Under the title "Parents", I wrote:

> Are parents "cracked"? True it is that we must have parents. At first they are loving, loveable people, at least mine were – they were adorable. Then suddenly it seems, I wasn't as loveable, and neither were they. What happened? I began to grow.
>
> I went to school, met other kids, began to learn about the world. I was big now, exactly three feet, one inch tall. Life

was bearable, but everyone said "no" when I wanted to help them. Then I turned eight.

By this time my mother thought I should perhaps do something around the house, like dusting some furniture. I did, but I still wanted to do more. But my darling mother said, "No".

Two or three years went by and my mother began to ask me to do things. I said, "No". I was "getting back", although it was subconsciously. Then my father intervened. He said I had to. So after a bit of difference, I learned to do "as I was told". No more asking.

Now I was a lazy, good-for-nothing teenage girl. But was it my fault; after all I had asked to help, my "puis-je vous aider" childhood had gone because everyone said "no".

Child psychology is the order of the day, surely someone knew about it then. My parents didn't, but the trouble is they still say, "no".

I'm not really rebellious, but "no" is such a final, sickening word and "yes" with "if you want to" is not exactly much better. Honestly, I love my parents and they love me, "to pieces" one might say, but that's it; I want to be whole. Parents never say "yes" or "no" at the right times and "if you like" far too much. Yet, I guess, having only one set of parents, I shouldn't generalise, I apologise, but I am an ordinary teenager (I hope) or at least not too unordinary so I must have ordinary parents.

Now I plead to the teenagers of the world, what is the solution to this problem? Do parents need parent psychologists? I think they do, in fact more than we need the child variety. Help us, psychologist, save us from these parental ogres we love."

I had no memory of this article. The fact that it was never discussed at school or at home does not amaze me but confirms the lack of connection and discussion in which I lived. Is it ironic that I trained many parents in many different parenting skills throughout my life as a volunteer and then as a school counsellor, or is this confirmation that I was on the path of destiny, driven by the motivation to heal my childhood wounds? I had forgotten what I knew about some aspects of the quality of my relationship with my parents.

Looking back on my childhood, I recognise I had been very lonely. It has taken me some time to identify the anxiety that accompanied that. My sister is only fourteen months younger than me, so there seems no obvious reason for having been lonely. I remember earlier times when we were playmates, and we dressed our dolls. We made cubby houses beneath upturned chairs that leaned against the wooden paling fence at our aunt's home, where we lived before our parents built a house, none too small a feat given the lack of home building resources in Australia at the end of the Second World War.

A few years ago, a number of things occurred, and my sister missed attending a series of events that were important to me. I felt devastated. It seems very silly I reacted so emotionally. I tried to make sense of this. It wasn't until a colleague told me it wasn't about me but about my sister that I began to unravel the problem.

I looked at our childhood from my sister's perspective. I wondered what it must have been like for her when her sister was taken off to hospital and she didn't see me for ten days, and when she did maybe I was not able to play, or I was different. Maybe she was told to leave me alone or not disturb me. I don't know, and neither does she. Then we moved and I was not much fun, as I stayed home for two months recuperating from scarlet fever, and she found a little soul mate across the road and had moved on. She was only five and doesn't remember but I do.

Three months before my eighth birthday, the day of our nana's funeral, we were each scheduled for a tonsillectomy. It was decided that my sister should have the operation to keep me company, despite having no symptoms. Researching the hospital where this occurred, I doubt my parents had any idea the family doctor was part of the consortium that owned it. My mother did not consider there was any problem in our having an operation that day. It would have been inconvenient to try to change it. Watching my father cry was disturbing, and I am unsure I knew why he was crying. Mum was rather indifferent to people grieving for parents who died when the children were adults. She thought they should be grateful they had them alive as long as they had. It wasn't as though they really needed them anymore. Her lack of empathy for people is something I have struggled to recognise of late.

I had problems with bleeding and was kept in hospital longer than my sister, and at home, after haemorrhaging, I returned to hospital for a blood transfusion. Maybe when my sister was playing around my bed and I sat up and vomited everywhere it freaked her out, and she didn't want to play with me? She remembers she was bustled away.

Months later, when I was eight, I waited for her at recess at school to cross the line when I expected her to be moved up from the infants' school to third grade in primary school. The line was painted on the asphalt, separating the playground for the older children from the younger ones. She never came, as her whole class repeated. It seems they were all considered too young to be promoted. This had some considerable effect on her self-esteem too.

I don't know. I hadn't moved on. Sixty years later I was still waiting for my little sister to want to play with me. This thought came unbidden as I drove 1,000 kilometres (620 miles) from my cousins' family reunion back home. My sister was a bubbly, outgoing child. I was not.

I doubt my mother comprehended I was lonely or anxious. She believed we were home together and did not know my sister wandered around the neighbourhood looking for friends. When I tried to play with the next-door neighbour, I was told I was not to go in there and bother her mother. I had the impression I was not good enough. They were richer than we were. They had one child and a bigger house that sat on a block twice as large as others in the street. The neighbour offered to sell a strip ten feet wide to my parents. My father often bemoaned that he had not taken up the offer as it would have provided enough space for a garage to be built beside the house.

I was far too anxious to have any confidence to continue to venture out to seek friendship and tried to be very good to win my parents' approval. Being very good meant following the rules laid down for me. Like any seven-year-old child, what was right and wrong was whatever my parents said. This is the first stage of moral development, as developed by Lawrence Kohlberg.

Having lost the security of my parents' presence and attunement to my needs at that age sheds some light on and understanding of my drive for Bible reading as I sought an authority to guide me. My parents paid for the subscription for the "Daily Bread" readings, thus transferring their authority to the advice given in the commentaries. To continue my emotional and moral growth, as is normal, I sought rules to guide me so people would like me. There was never any discussion about what I was reading.

I read and did my homework. What else was there to do? Television was still a new phenomenon in Australia, and programming was very limited. There were few books, with no library nearby. I avidly read the monthly *School Magazine* from cover to cover. I never had a bicycle, as my mother learned to drive a car when I was nine or ten and became very conscious and afraid of children on the roads riding their bikes. Rather than teach us how to ride safely, she chose that we would never have bikes. I rode my first bike at the age of thirty-two, but the laughter of my children at my wobbliness and fear was not conducive to my taking it up with much gusto. I haven't attempted to ride for decades.

The summer I turned eleven, I wore a cardigan for months, even though it was extremely hot, because my arms were covered in hives. I guess Mum never saw them. I was in pyjamas when she went to work and when she returned at six in the evening. By the time my first boyfriend appeared, when I was not quite fifteen, I was more than ready to have someone who could spend time with me.

At the end of my fifteenth year, I became quite stressed about a state-wide external examination, the results of which determined the recipients of a scholarship to stay at school to complete high school. I developed severe acne that was never treated by a doctor. My mother's comment was she didn't understand why I should have pimples as neither she nor my father had. The following year my eyes were tested, and I was found to be extremely short-sighted. My mother made a similar comment about my need to wear glasses when neither she nor my dad did. These two factors further reduced my self-esteem.

This contributed to the set of beliefs and thoughts that formed the paradigm for my relationships. When it came to discussing health issues I was unable to be assertive about health problems or to adequately discuss them as I expected other people to respond in similar ways to my mother, for them to mirror my mother's attitude to my health. Indeed, considering IBS, constipation, poor eyesight, skin problems, asthma and other physical problems already discussed, her attitude to my physical and psychological well-being was dismissive and created in me the expectation that they were insignificant, undeserving of consideration and demonstrably my fault.

Prior to sitting the externally set exam held two years later at the end of high school, I again suffered stress, experiencing a strange giggling, hysterical episode at school some weeks before the examination period. My teacher told me to relax and take a break! She suggested I had been studying too much.

My parents were unable to bridge the sense of abandonment I suffered as a very sick child left alone in hospital. My mother always said I was so deep. I had been traumatised and from my adult perspective I recognise that many symptoms I had are also those of depression such as feelings of sadness, fear of rejection, low energy and fatigue, guilt, worthlessness, lack of interest and ability to participate in outside activities and social withdrawal. They are also well explained by my experiences. I looked for companionship that involved communication, although there remained an inability to ask for what I needed, and an acceptance of denial of what I wanted, an acceptance that I should be compliant. Such was part of the paradigm for all my relationships. If there was talking and physical closeness, I believed that was all that was possible.

Even in friendships my expectations were very low. In the early years of high school, I listened to another girl's fantastic stories about her boyfriend. Another classmate queried me about whether or not I believed the tales. It did not matter to me. She was talking with me. We sat near each other. She is dead now. She died in her mid-thirties.

I couldn't understand my childhood without understanding my parents. This led me from my adult perspective to understand many of my own attitudes and choices too. I became more aware of the many decisions that had been the basis of my life. It assisted me in making sense of it.

My father was a hard worker, obtaining his own unskilled job at fourteen, having left school against his mother's wishes. Excluding his time as a soldier, he stayed with the same firm for his entire working life of forty-six years, first as a delivery driver for thirty years, which kept him physically fit, which was just as well since the only sport he ever played was snooker.

He was a beer-drinking affable Australian male who took up smoking as a young soldier and never gave it up. He loved going to the RSL[12] clubs and was a loyal mate. He had an assured demeanour, was honest, and cleanliness, neatness, and doing things right the first

[12] The Returned and Services League of Australia is the organisation for support of those who have served or are serving in Australia's Defence Forces.

time were important values for him. He was a handyman about the house. He kept the house well maintained and the garden trim and tidy. On a recent nostalgic visit to my childhood home the grassed area in the backyard compared poorly with the Sir Walter Scott Buffalo lawn my father had mown and edged so carefully.

I never saw him cook except on the barbeque. He had a great memory, tremendous spatial skills, was good with numbers, always read the daily newspaper but never a book, was an avid TV news watcher, and went early to bed and was early to rise, being intolerant of people keeping other hours. He never quite appreciated that being woken at five thirty in the morning with a cup of tea when I visited them was not the wonderful gift he intended, especially if I had been awake many times breastfeeding a baby.

To state that the only male I really knew was my father is tremendously challenging. I knew so little about my father that using the verb "knew" contradicts its meaning. Without close contact with male cousins; none with the strange boy next door; no boys in any class after the age of seven until I went to university; no brothers; a distant, unknown grandfather; and rare visits with uncles, one would think I was ill-prepared to find a mate. The boys at university amazed me. In lecture theatres that stacked five hundred university students, tier upon tier, I was astounded to see them shoot paper aeroplanes toward the lecturer.

When I considered what the negative aspects of my father's character that affected me the most were, I remembered his moodiness and bad temper. My mother excused him from this as being caused by his working so hard and being very tired. He would work overtime three nights each week and not arrive home until nine in the evening, which was after I was in bed asleep, so until I was in high school, I mostly saw him briefly in the mornings, when he would kiss us good-bye, and on the weekends. Even though he was affable and kissed everyone, I don't remember any other physical affection after the age of six. Affection was ritualised for him with us, with kissing on arrival home and on leaving.

My father never praised me, and at sixteen, when I was dux of my high school, I was not given any form of acknowledgement. I even asked what a person had to do around here to get some praise. He never praised any achievement or acknowledged any effort. Until I was twelve, I was involved in concerts for physical culture. He would time my performance and bemoan the amount of time required for making costumes and practice for the three minutes spent on stage.

Attendance at my hockey games when I was fifteen was unimaginable. I always had to make my own way there via two buses and a train and walking. My mother told me years later that my father was inordinately proud of me and would tell all his friends how well I was doing. I never heard a word from him.

As a teenager, I went ballroom dancing but was never allowed to compete for medals as it was too expensive. I loved ballroom dancing, but my father could not dance. Spending those years between eighteen and twenty-two in jungles in New Guinea and Borneo during the Second World War wasn't conducive to practising the waltz or tango. I suppose I accepted married couples didn't dance.

His war service was never discussed. At the end of his life, he commented on racing back on his Harley-Davidson from behind the enemy lines. He was a despatch rider, and though he had thought he might enjoy riding a motorbike on his return to Australia, he decided fairly quickly that he was not interested. He experienced a crash in an aeroplane, being cushioned from harm by the bags of mail they were carrying. Looking back, and knowing about PTSD, his drinking and smoking were ways he coped with his feelings. His temper possibly was more related to his war service than being tired.

Dad was obsessively neat; if I left a pair of shoes at the end of my bed, I would be criticised for leaving my bedroom a mess. From my perspective now as a psychologist, his behaviour looks like a symptom of OCD (obsessive-compulsive disorder) connected with anxiety from PTSD. When I was nine or ten, I remember my mother had spent all day polishing the floors and furniture. He came home and ran his finger along the mantelpiece, criticising her for the dust left there. My mother went to work after that, stating there was no point in her staying home if it wasn't going to be appreciated. All the other mothers in the street stayed at home. By the time I was in high school, I did all the vacuuming and dusting each week.

During childhood, we occasionally went on picnics on the weekends and were sent to the Saturday afternoon cinema and to Sunday school. I don't remember my parents playing with us, except once when I was fourteen and we were on one of our rare holidays in Queensland. It was raining, so dad taught us Euchre. We bet pennies and lost. He laughed when I wanted my pennies returned, as it was "for keeps." If we went on holidays, it was in March, during school term, for a fortnight. We did this even in my final year. There was no concern about me missing two weeks of study. I was expected to keep up with my schoolwork on my own.

On my sixteenth birthday, I arrived home from my holiday job at the city department store where my father had worked all his life. Everyone had eaten dinner. Mine was being slowed dried out over a boiling, water-filled saucepan under a lid. I ate by myself while the other three sat watching television. I thought turning sweet sixteen was supposed to be something special. There were songs written about it.

In high school, once I wanted to go on a three day excursion, I was told no, as we did not have the money, so I never asked again. When my younger sister went on a similar trip, amazingly I voiced how very hurt I felt. They said, "we wondered why you never went on any …" with the explanation, "Oh, but that was at that time, not forever." This was a lesson that questioning my parents did not remedy the situation. Being assertive after the fact was useless. This was mirrored in my early marriage as I accepted there was a lack of money for whenever I wanted something.

I was glad I didn't have to ask to finish high school. My teachers had contacted my parents suggesting it. My mum had wanted to complete high school but had not been allowed, so they were pleased to allow me, as long as they never had to ask me about doing my homework. Of course they knew they wouldn't need to ask.

My father's emotional distance from me was my normal. I had no emotional intimacy with anyone. Even if I felt I was missing out on something, it had no label. It was in books, in love stories, in other people, but it was all fiction.

Mum was overweight, but when I look at photos, she was plump but not as obese as both my sister and I became, yet we believed she was fat at the time. She was intelligent, good with figures, a hard worker, faithful, serious, independent, self-sufficient, friendly, and a good friend. She could argue well and prided herself on knowing things. She would talk to anyone, telling them her life story in the first half hour of meeting them, and hated silence in conversations.

Focused on my father, she always sought to please her husband. She was an attentive, caring aunt, a fact I never appreciated until I took over her Christmas card list after her death, when I received copious notes about her from my cousins. I believe this stemmed from the fact that she first became an aunt at the age of nine, shortly after her mother's death. She would, however, cut people off, including her father, sister, and some friends, for relatively small matters or misunderstandings and not speak to them for many years. It frequently seemed that it was twelve years before she approached a person to mend the rupture.

When she first met Dad, she told him she was different from other girls, as she did not have a mother to protect her. He took this seriously. She reported he never pressured her for premarital sex, though his assertion that you couldn't tell if a slice was missing from a cut loaf casts his protection in a highly misogynistic light. She didn't really like her sisters and grew up intending to be different from the rest of her family. Considering my belief that I have swum against the tide throughout my life, I have emulated this same attitude, and I realise she affirmed my right to do this.

Unlike my father, when she left school at fourteen, it was at her family's insistence. Her much older eldest sister had raised her after their mother's death seven years earlier. Factory work had been good enough for her, so it was good enough for my mother. They needed her money to survive in 1938.

I loved reading. It was something at which I have always excelled. From the age of four I could read. Although I loved my mother reading Charles Kingsley's *The Water Babies*, I cannot remember many books in the house. They must have had some, as I inherited them. Maybe they were kept in a cupboard? However, looking at them on a shelf nearby, most appear to have been purchased later in the lives of my parents, after I had left home. Mum read women's magazines. We never visited a library. I don't believe there was one anywhere near us.

Discovering the library in high school remains one of my happiest memories. At lunchtime I would visit and choose books depending upon how thick they were, with the intention that reading them would last the evening. Looking at a photograph of the library in my school magazine, I am astounded by its sparseness and paucity of shelving. It bears little resemblance to the local libraries I now frequent and looks more like my home library.

My mother sat on a chair between our beds when she read to us. When I read to my children, it was always next to them with my arm around them. At ten years of age, I was missing from my birthday party, and found on the floor at the foot of my bed, reading one of the four books that had been given to me. Probably Porter's *Pollyanna*, which I have recently decided was a very unfortunate model for me. I have spent my life playing the glad game, always looking for the silver lining, reframing things to see the positive. Psychologists have built careers on positive psychology and cognitive behavioural therapy, reframing unhelpful thoughts into more helpful ones. However, I missed the significance of things that were negative.

It should not be a surprise that I took on many of her traits, although I thought many of my conscious choices were diametrically opposed to her attitudes. My mother always said that if my sister and I were drowning and so was Daddy, she would save him. Considering she couldn't swim until she chose to learn in her fifties, this was a surprising statement, but it reflected her emphasis on her relationship with my father. She often said when she met him, having lost her mother at such a young age, having been estranged from her father and her extended family, she had a lot of love to give and she gave it all to him.

This seemed perfectly reasonable, and I don't remember objecting. It was part of the whole scenario that I was not all that worthwhile and certainly not as important as my father. I guess that was why I decided not to focus on me but on my children. I did not want to be like my mother. Unfortunately for the adult me, it was as if my six-year-old self ended up choosing my partner. However, this was not a conscious choice. One of the reasons my mother gave for "saving Daddy if he was drowning" and not her daughters was that we would grow up and leave her. Ironically, she came to live around the corner from me when she was a widow.

I never saw my mother play, but I believe she had been a good piano player. Despite this my mother never thought to have us taught. I daresay it was too expensive. I was forbidden from playing a neighbour's piano. Thus when Dan, who was an accomplished guitarist, only ever expected me to watch him but would never show me the simplest chord, it felt quite normal. I didn't like being an audience. It was very boring and I refused to do it. There were more interesting things to do on a Saturday with my newborn than care for him on a hot summer's day in a garage noisy with a bunch of musicians jamming. I accepted that I was not good enough to teach and not worthy of the patience it would require, but I at least asserted my right to care for my baby in more comfortable surroundings and spent the day with my in-laws or at home.

My mother also was a regular churchgoer and tennis player, activities she relinquished when she married. I emulated her here too, never playing netball again, nor following through with a dramatics club or dancing.

Each week, Mum wrote out the order for George's local grocery store. This was in the era when there literally were corner shops, as there was at the end of my street and the next street too. My father would pick up the order on the way home. I never saw my mother bring home the grocery shopping, so it seemed normal that Dan should do the grocery shopping, even though all the women I knew did theirs, devoting a whole day to it, having lunch with a friend or coffee along the way. The effect on me was that I accepted I had little access to money when I left teaching to raise a family. I also had no opportunity to meet with friends over lunch.

Access to Bankcard, the forerunner of credit cards in the mid seventies when it was first introduced gave some relief though I don't remember feeling free to use it except in an emergency. I used the Child Endowment, and then the Family Allowance that replaced it in 1976 to pay for sewing materials and knitting wool and shoes for the children. The more children I had the larger the payment. In 1976 the payment for three children was $14.50, which today would be worth $85. I guess it was thought that was enough to provide for clothing for them and me. Looking at old family photos I notice the hand made clothes.

In a recent photographic retrospective of the local branch of the CWL, I look a little dowdy beside other members. Perhaps they were more skilled than I or could afford to buy clothes. It was useful that my sister-in-law would send her discarded clothes and those of my nieces across to us. She bought beautiful clothes but unfortunately we were very different body types. I admit to feelings of resentment rather than gratitude.

My mother always chose my sister for the task of buying some fruit at George's, as I never brought home the best specimens. Reviewing this, I realise it was because I was quite short-sighted. This does not make any difference in a modern setting in the local supermarket where I pick out the fruit myself, but in the 1950s, all the fruit and vegetables were behind the grocer, who stood behind his counter. I did not point out the best fruit, because I could not see the blemishes. I am sure George should have been a little more ethical in his dealings with a ten-year-old.

I wonder how much this belief of my not being any good at picking out fresh fruit and vegetables contributed to my acceding to not being the grocery shopper, which was an important factor in the lack of financial independence that occurred in the early years of marriage. As well, other women, who found the task burdensome, frequently congratulated me. They told me how marvellous it must be for me not to need to take toddlers shopping.

However, with my youngest child now in his thirties, there have been many years when that would not have been a problem! Indeed, when using self-catering holiday accommodation I enjoyed planning the menu and shopping for the week's groceries. I was dismayed when, on returning to Australia, the old pattern reasserted itself, and I was relegated once again to being told an item was not on the list, or that we did not need to be subjected to impulse buying.

Having been buying my own groceries now for more than two years, I have to admit to still being thrilled by it. A small independence, it is true, but one I value. I buy fillet steak and marinated Tasmanian salmon, fresh vegetables, chicken fillets, and smoked salmon for breakfast. I never buy cheap cuts of meat, like mince or chuck steak, and out-of-date goods are not put into my shopping trolley. I realise too how little time it actually requires. I have been surprised that I can leave and return in just over half an hour when Dan required at least two hours (normally much more). If I had accompanied Dan to do the weekly grocery shopping, he would not have had the many hours to himself that he had. Of course there was nothing wrong with him having that time to himself. I just did not realise at the time that it was happening.

As little girls, we were never permitted to enter our parents' bedroom, not even if ill. It was with some shock I returned one evening when my eldest was six months old after leaving him with my parents to be babysat, to find his bassinet empty. A quiet voice called out, "He's in here with us." Tucked up between my parents was my precious child, in a place I had never been. I remember finding it hard to cross the threshold to pick him up! "But I was never allowed in," I said, and it was acknowledged it was thus.

Though with our first child, I did not take him with me to bed to breastfeed, later babies were able to explore the comforts of the family bed. Our youngest would still slip in at the bottom of our bed even as an eleven-year-old. I took great delight in waking in the middle of the night to find a baby sleeping beside me, often because Dan had heard him stir and brought him in, even letting him nuzzle into me for a feed without waking me. Thankfully, breastfeeding did not cost anything.

With my children, breastfeeding created a physical closeness that I missed as they weaned. I did not know how to talk with babies, and I sometimes wondered if my eldest child's early struggles with language were in part due to my lack of conversation with him though he was traumatised by his hospitalisation, which is sufficient to account for a problem with his normal development. I confess I would allow him to suckle for an hour while I immersed myself in a book. This was not a problem with subsequent children, as I was always too busy with an older toddler to be bothered with a book. There was little time for reading when the children were awake. Emotional closeness created through shared conversations of dreams and fears was not fostered as much as it could have been in the struggle to impose morals upon them. I could only create what I knew, though I hoped to have done better.

As a child, I accepted how I was parented was the normal way parents showed love. After all, I was well fed, clothed by the efforts of my mother's sewing and knitting, well housed in a neat and clean environment, and educated beyond what my parents had experienced. I was not abused physically or sexually and never thought I was emotionally abused either. It is only in the last ten years I have questioned this about my childhood and found recently that my sister attests to what was tantamount to emotional neglect, as she too has re-evaluated her childhood.

The rules were not inconsistent and did not change depending upon the mood of either parent. My medical needs were met. I was taken to the dentist, although with both the doctor and the dentist, the cost of providing anaesthetic for removal of a tooth or a plantar wart was deemed too great, and I suffered through the experiences.

It was interesting discussing the cost of dental anaesthetic with another baby boomer as I helped her overcome her anxiety in preparation for a dental appointment. Like me, she had endured the dental drill without pain relief.

I was taught how to knit and sew and clean house. I was not taught how to intimately connect with any other human being, this despite my parents, as a couple and individually having a fairly solid network of friends. Learning about attachment theory, beginning with John Bowlby when I was at university in the sixties, I thought I had a secure attachment as an infant. My mother always tut-tutted about any of her relatives that bottle fed their infants by propping the bottle up on a pillow as she always insisted she held me and would carry me around in a baby sling device (which she called a cuddle seat). If she was attuned to me as a little one, I don't believe she was able to overcome the loss of attunement from her own mother when she lost her at age seven.

My emotional security was shattered at six and a half, as after hospitalisation my parents were no longer able to reassure me. I learned through illness that I could and would elicit care. For instance, earache caused me to whimper in the middle of the night, and Mum would come in to pat my head. I believe isolated touch became very important as a result, so much so that I did not expect much physical touching, but it increased in importance because it was rare and required elicitation from me. Touch that was freely offered was more powerful as a result.

I asked my mother not long before she died if ever she was afraid for me when I couldn't breathe, or was sick, crying, haemorrhaging, and rushed to hospital, and she said, "Yes, of course, but I never let you know. I would worry and be upset outside the room when I was away from you." I think she was mistaken—she did let me know, and it was in her eyes. I think I withdrew because I didn't know the meaning of what I saw.

Paradoxically, being sick was unacceptable, and fear provoking. Children only know concrete things, not abstract values. I couldn't think, *Oh, Mum is worried that I'm sick. She loves me so much and feels powerless to make me better and is not sure what to do, so she is worried.* Even if I could have done so, I am sure I would have believed it was my fault I was sick, which would be enough to explain the look in her eyes.

Perhaps she could have softened her eyes and let me see her love, not her fear, let me see her confidence in me, my body, to become well, to heal, to get over it.

Working It Through

Here are three ways of discovering more about your childhood. Many people believe they do not remember their childhood very well, but using these methods, you may discover something that relates to your present issues.

Perhaps every time you ask for something that is important to you, there is no time to discuss it. Perhaps it is whenever you would like to see a movie, or visit friends, or plan a holiday—your preference is somehow never the one chosen. Perhaps you would like another child, or to move to the country, or to be closer to your relatives or further away? You may focus on your relationship with your spouse, a sibling, a friend, a child, or a parent. Identify what in the relationship is missing or causing you distress.

What causes you pain? It may be a behaviour to which you react with distress in your relationship. Such behaviour may be someone's abuse of alcohol, gambling, spending, hoarding, shopping, use of pornography, obsessive behaviour, a habit, or over-commitment to an institution like a club, church, a sport, or a hobby.

Look at your reactions to which behaviours in the relationship are causing you the most pain now.

- Is the present issue in a relationship? With whom? You may focus on your relationship with your spouse, a sibling, a friend, a child, or a parent.
- Is there a behaviour that is a problem? Whose?
- Is there a sensation in your body that causes you distress? Where? When does this occur?
- Is there an emotion that you experience that is disturbing? What is it? When does it occur?

Touchstone Event

There was a pivotal point of change in my relationship with my parents and this may be the case for you. Look for the earliest memory that defines a relationship with a parent, or perhaps a memory stands out to define it. This may be a memory that relates to your present issue.

Of course, the relationship with your parents may have been a constant. There will be an earliest memory of the difficulties you experienced. Perhaps it is when you were five, and your father destroyed your little books and paintings when your mother enrolled you in a private school against his wishes. Perhaps it was as a three-year-old, as you sat on a swing with your mother and your mother continually asked, "Who are you and where do you belong?" It continues until you feel that your answer is wrong and unacceptable and so are you. Maybe it is later, when you are six, and your mother stands there with her bags packed ready to leave, saying, "Now you will learn what it is like not to have a mother." Then you spend decades trying fruitlessly to gain her approval.

Whether a memory surfaced that was pivotal, or was the earliest memory where you can identify the emotional pain, or was a memory of a constant theme, you can continue to identify its impact on you by noting the body sensations created when you immerse yourself in the memory, or by your reaction to a current issue.

Float back in your imagination through your years, down your timeline. How do you feel? What sensations do you experience as you think of this relationship? Close your eyes, and take the time to be in touch with those sensations. Write them down in a notebook or type them on your computer. Record them on your phone, but don't let them swirl around in your head, because you will need to recall them to undertake the work you need to do.

Note other times these feelings were there; these body sensations will connect you with those memories. You don't need to force it. Just notice. Then keep going back, into your childhood, to find that touchstone event.

Dr. Francine Shapiro defined the touchstone event when she developed EMDR therapy. It was when the "little you" first learned something that you have not processed or unlearned. It is vivid. People remember amazing details, such as what they were wearing, the colour of the cereal bowl, how high above the their head was the table, the weather, the time of day. Describe that first time to yourself. Really place yourself there. Keep your eyes closed, imagine the surroundings, and picture the people, the events, the sounds, the smells, the body sensations, the emotions, the chatter in your head, what you are hearing and seeing.

Childhood memories should not remain distressing. They are in the past. They are not the present. If they remain disturbing, and you cannot reduce the distress to zero, seek professional help as you deserve to be happy without childhood debris clogging up your view! Desensitize yourself on any of the memories that remain disturbing. Use progressive relaxation (see chapter 1), EMDR therapy, journaling, or meditation.

Chapter 6

ON THE OTHER SIDE OF SIXTEEN

In the magnificent great hall at the university with hundreds of others, I sat frozen for ten minutes. At the end of my first year at university, I had no words to describe the hammer-beam roof, or the carvings, statues, or stained-glass window set high above my head. Overwhelmed, I was required to write six essays for my psychology examination. Minutes into the exam, I was unable to spell "were," wondering what "were" actually meant! Now I can recognise the freeze response I was experiencing that numbed my brain. I prayed. The simple act of prayer, of slowly breathing, calmed me sufficiently to reduce the panic attack and allowed me to complete the exam and pass.

The following year, at eighteen, I became engaged to marry. I walked toward my father with great trepidation, his back to me. I said, "He has asked me to marry him and I said yes." He didn't say a word, and many years later my mother told me my father was dumbstruck. There was no discussion about emotions, or plans, or what this meant. There was no congratulations, or even a comment that I was far too young to make such a decision, despite a niggling belief I held that I was. After all, I wasn't halfway through my course at university, he was my first boyfriend, and I should not have been closing off options. Perhaps since my parents had met at eighteen, in the months prior to my father being conscripted into the army, they believed I was old enough.

I had doubts about becoming engaged but naively believed that as we were sexually active, it was as good as if we were married. This is an obvious rationalisation. If someone proposed, you accepted. I agreed to marriage because I was asked, and now I wonder if it was based on guilt over sex. Like many in my generation, I had been taught and believed only "bad" girls had sex. It was never implied that only "bad" boys were involved as the double standard was embedded in the culture, and feminism's challenge to the patriarchal society had not arrived anywhere near where I lived. The freedom that the oral contraceptive would eventually confer on females had not penetrated far enough either into the culture of the 1960s to counter the upbringing of the conservative teen baby boomer.

I broke that first engagement a year later. My parents never asked for an explanation. In fact, unbeknownst to me, my ex-fiancé would call around and visit my mother every afternoon, pleading with her to intervene and make me go back to him. Communication was not a strong point in our family. My mother didn't mention this until many years later, but simultaneously, she scarcely spoke to me. It took me six months to question this, at which point I felt compelled to ask her why she wasn't talking to me, declaring that surely she thought I might have had good reason to break up with him. It is as though it had to build up inside me until I could no longer contain the question. It was a style of communication that dominated my relationships. It reappeared when being open did not work later in my marriage.

Each morning and evening I walked twenty minutes to the local train station to go to university. There was a rough track that commuters had worn through the area that was undeveloped next to the boys' high school. One sunny morning, in my second year, while enjoying the smell of the eucalyptus and the feel of the crunch of gravel, I was shocked to feel hands wrenching up my skirt at my underwear. I turned around screaming at a young dark-haired man with such indignation that he let go of me, stumbled backward, and fled.

Shaken, I stood there momentarily before deciding I was nearer the station than home. In any case, no one was at home, and my girlfriend would be expecting me to catch her train. I knew I would feel safer in her presence. That night I related my experience to my parents. There was no reaction except to phone a family friend who was a sergeant of police to report it. They did not advise any change in my routine, or ever in four years of my attending university and travelling home after dark did they offer to pick me up from the train station.

My mother told me about her sister smacking her across the face when she reported a neighbour tried to force his way into their home when she was fourteen. I guess that was as far as her empathy was able to go. However it felt like her experience was much more significant and it belittled me and had the effect of shutting down the discussion.

Years later, when a family member disclosed being molested, I was as puzzled by the lack of response and support shown by others, but it too mirrored what I had experienced from my parents. I found it very confusing too when I shared my distress with my parish priest. The perpetrator actually would approach me at Mass to be given communion when I was on the roster as a Eucharistic minister. The priest's advice was for me to take myself off the roster. No assistance was offered for the distress anyone was feeling despite my requesting it. I believe it would be handled very differently now.

In August during my third year at university, I broke that first engagement because I was more aware of who I was and how incompatible we were. He was a tradesman who mocked me if I expressed any opinion, asking me where had I read that, as if reading was equivalent to being an idiot. He had done very poorly at school himself and defended himself by belittling me as my education continued. He did not want me to go to university and did not want me to become a teacher. He told my parents they shouldn't let me go to university, but when they did, he planned to pay out the bond I had as a condition of accepting my scholarship to university so I would not go out teaching.

As a contrast, at university, a young fellow named Daniel talked with me about things in which I was interested. His foot had accidentally touched my leg during a tutorial, and I had felt an instant electric shock. He was otherwise involved, and I didn't expect he would actually be interested in me romantically, but I couldn't marry someone else when so little excited me so much.

I was delighted that someone wanted to converse about religion with me and about the traditions of the Catholic Church. My nana had been Catholic. I am now trying to absorb the fact that if my father had been a traditional Catholic, and not one who stated, "I only went to Mass during the war to get out of KP duty," I may have been interested in an atheist!

Months later, Dan was no longer in a relationship. He told me that he always felt insecure with her, as she was so beautiful. When I told a priest in 2014 about this, he expressed surprise that I had not been insulted, but I had not noticed! As university students, I accepted there was no money, so studying and walking were how we spent our time. It was wonderful being able to talk. I felt special and interesting and not lonely.

My girlfriend had met her future husband by this time, so she was involved with her boyfriend. Dan and I would meet in the university's library and study together. I enjoyed the conversation and physical closeness, though I now realise I was misinterpreting it for emotional intimacy, about which I had no real concept.

My first boyfriend had not appreciated my spirituality. Wanting to go on a picnic and impatient for me to leave church, he sent in an elder to ask me to come outside. With a tiny congregation of fifty or fewer at my local Presbyterian Church, it was of no little embarrassment to me to be hauled out! I thought someone must have died. The first time Daniel asked me to go anywhere with him, though it was not a date, was on the Assumption of Our Lady to attend Mass at a beautiful church in the city. Once there, I fainted. I had not eaten. I remember thinking it was some spiritual sign.

It appeared to me he shared many of my father's positive traits. Talking and touch was all I required. As well as being a good driver, hard worker, fit and healthy, he was not completely as traditional in his expectations of the male role within the house, as I saw him wipe dishes at his parents' home and be helpful in various ways. He believed girls should be educated. He did not smoke or drink, having signed a pledge not to do so until he turned twenty-one, but it was illegal to drink under the age of twenty-one in that era in Australia.

However, two months after his twenty-first birthday, Daniel wrote asking me to help him to give up drinking after he had vomited up all the contents of the pub-crawl the night before. His pattern of drinking mirrored what I had seen in my childhood. It was a very common pattern that I would see replicated in my children's generation. Coming of age for Australian boys seemed to demand becoming paralytic with mates. My mother tolerated my father's binge drinking. Initially it related to his attendance at Anzac Day marches and reunions with his Second World War army mates.

In later years, my mother asked my father's oncologist about his advice concerning alcohol consumption. The doctor had advised not having more than two a day. My mother asked him if he meant two glasses of beer, two schooners, two "long-necks", (three pints) or two jugs (four pints)? My father was still consuming two jugs of home-brewed beer on a daily basis, despite being on steroids for treatment of lymphocytic leukaemia.

In the '60s and '70s, it seemed to me that men were expected to drink and smoke. I didn't know any that didn't. It was not a surprise to me when after a night celebrating our first wedding anniversary with our parents and friends, with copious amounts of beer and wine served with the soup, fish and dessert, my father-in-law finished the evening by filling his coffee cup three times with Drambuie. The sweet, golden coloured liqueur was 40% alcohol made from scotch whiskey, honey, herbs and spices.

I now doubt the accuracy of the tale as it seems impossible but while I was home-birthing my last child, when barbequing for his grandchildren, my father-in-law drank twelve "long-necks" in one evening. As this would have entailed his consuming nine litres or two gallons of beer, I wonder if it was a story that grew, like the fish that "got away" increases in size with the retelling. It was considered an amazing feat rather than ever condemned. This sorry state of an alcoholic's addiction reflected the family environment and values. Looking through the eyes of a clinician, his unfortunate childhood experiences and the dangers of his service in the armed forces during the Second World War add understanding to their protective and indulgent attitude.

One foggy winter's night I woke up on the highway median strip at three in the morning. I had fallen asleep in the passenger seat, as had my two eldest children, who were then a breastfeeding baby and a toddler. In the seventies there were no seatbelts and no consternation about driving home after a night out partying. I did not feel we were safe but awareness of the dangers was limited.

In that era, blokes would help a mate unable to stagger from the pub into his car so he could drive home! By law, hotel bars had to close at 6 o' clock and there was a phenomenon called the "six o' clock swill" wherein all the pub patrons would order more beer just before closing. I was always grateful that Dan never frequented hotels or took part in such ritualistic inebriation.

I rarely saw Daniel display anger, and he appeared even-tempered, was assured, not obsessive about neatness or cleanliness, and so was very attractive to me, as he did not display some of the traits I disliked in my father. Dan was many things my father wasn't, being university-educated, a committed "churchgoer," interested in discussing things, and a non-smoker. He was not a dark and brooding handsome Brontë "Heathcliff" like my father.

A shock of ginger hair atop his short stocky frame, with pale grey eyes contrasted with my dad. In the inimitable Australian paradox, his nickname was "Bluey", an irritating nonsense made more so in later years when friends of my sons would ring asking for "Blue" or "Bluey" and I would respond with "which one?"

We were able to discuss our assignments and essays. He seemed a mature, quiet boy with whom I would sit and study in the university library. Catching a glimpse of him among the book stacks sent my little heart aquiver. With the pale skin he inherited from his Jutland ancestors, he could not enjoy the Australian sun the way my father and I could with our Mediterranean olive complexions. He was more like my mother in complexion. On her honeymoon she endured extremely bad sunburn when they went fishing all day in a boat near Mandurah. Prior to his being demobbed from the army, Dad had asked her not to become suntanned as he wanted to enjoy seeing her pale skin after his years in Borneo and New Guinea.

Dan had extraordinarily long fingers for such a short man, which he used to great effect with the guitar, a fact I didn't appreciate at 2 am when he serenaded me with Dylan's "Lay, Lady Lay". I had only just gone to sleep having been kept awake with a very colicky baby. It probably provided the seed for the family myth that mum didn't like music.

Given my father's lack of verbal encouragement, any lack of words of praise, encouragement, or compliments was normal. Weird statements about my eyes being like rocks that needed interpretation from the geologist he was, explaining about gold flecks in black obsidian, were the closest I experienced to a compliment. Any complaint that something wasn't a compliment was greeted with a shrug. The children came to say, "That's just Dad."

As the months progressed, my brain continued its healing journey. It has taken time, but I have realised the complete truth of anxiety being the connecting emotion from childhood through young adulthood through my marriage until now. When I was dating in the late 1960s, I was never certain how long the relationship was going to last. It was an on again/off again relationship.

Anxiety was not something I suffered only in relationships. When I went out teaching at twenty, I became very anxious. There were no other females on the mathematics faculty. The mathematics head teacher took me to the mathematics staff room, looked in, and told me how unsuitable it would be for me, and proceeded further down the corridor to the arts/home economics staffroom with the women. Certainly I did not feel I could object. It played into my belief of "I am not good enough."

I had little support in teaching mathematics. I could not return to the mathematics staff room to discuss issues after a class with my fellow teachers. I was required to queue up with the naughty year nine boys, waiting patiently until they had had "six of the best"[13] before I could talk to the head teacher. I felt belittled. I did not deserve to be with the other mathematics teachers.

The arts/home economics staff had quite different management issues, with their practical classes restricted to twenty girls, as the boys would be scheduled for metal work or woodwork. In contrast to the mathematics teachers, I remember their names and details of their families. They must have acquiesced to the provision of space in their staffroom for me, thus accepting the hierarchy's decision that I belonged there. This further reinforced the appropriateness of his actions that were appallingly misogynistic.

A couple of years later my girlfriend was transferred to the same high school, and having far better esteem than I, knew better than to accept such relegation to the women's quarters. Unlike me, she had been raised with brothers and was at ease with male behaviour in a way I never was. Classroom management came easily to her.

The rattling of the train, its swaying as we held on to supporting straps hanging from the ceiling, the smell of tobacco smoke, the

[13] Corporal punishment, through the administration of six cuts on the hand by a cane, termed caning, was still legal in state Department of Education schools at this time.

smoke curling into the air throughout the carriage, the rustle of newspaper broadsheets being folded and refolded, the heat of bodies packed into the crowded commuter train all provided the background to our conversation.

It's been fifty years since she befriended me at university. She talked with me, sitting close, sharing dreams, and was the first to expand my expectations of what a relationship could comprise. She supported me emotionally when I broke that first engagement, confiding that she always noticed my personality change the closer the train was to my stop. She had supported me when I feared a teenage pregnancy the year earlier.

Unfortunately, it took until 2013 for me to accept and reciprocate the depth and breadth of her friendship by fully sharing with her my inner life. This was understandable, as I had pushed so much out of my conscious awareness. I could not share what I did not know.

We very rarely met alone for lunch or even a coffee since we had married, despite living in the same cities, having shared our friendship as parts of couples except for the occasional phone call. After relaying the contents of any phone call comments like, "You must have talked about more than that," occurred. It felt like I had to justify the length of a phone call by relating enough information, whether this was from a friend, my sister or my mother.

This was reminiscent of my father, who would quickly demand I hang up if I remained talking on the telephone. We never had a phone until I was eighteen, as he refused to have it connected and considered it too expensive. The experience was repeated when I married, as the telephone was again considered too expensive to connect, despite it resulting in my being in labour with my second child without a means of telephoning for transport to the maternity wing of the hospital. It is only by good fortune that someone came to visit and I was able to request help.

After three weeks of marriage, I remarked to my bridegroom, when I saw him reading the newspaper while I was vacuuming the apartment that I had not thought I would be doing all the housework, as that was not what we had agreed we would do. He replied that his turn would come. Pregnancy and morning sickness soon brought home that reality for him, but I remember him rarely using the vacuum cleaner, and never in the latter years.

I should have put down the vacuum cleaner then and read the newspaper too. Instead, I condoned the implication that it was acceptable that he would only help when I was incapacitated and required assistance. This I never intended.

It seems so obvious now but I had never seen my father vacuum the house. I had done the vacuuming for my family since the age of twelve, so I accepted that it was my role, despite having written to Daniel how little I enjoyed doing household chores.

I accepted dividing chores along traditional gender lines, though as a newlywed I questioned it. The fact that I had maintained that belief was brought home to me when I noticed I was shocked when I actually saw my son-in-law vacuum their home.

I was aware of other couples sharing housework, but I accepted that if I did not do the housework, it would not be done. This was reinforced by Dan's comment after he retired that if he took over the vacuuming, I would not be doing anything. I was frustrated that I could not communicate the inherent unfairness of it as it was so ostensibly untrue, but it effectively maintained the status quo.

Part of the bargain of holidays in the last ten years for me was I would not make the beds on my own, though I was more than a little unhappy that this did not translate into help when we returned home.

While caring for three little kids, I went to the Accident and Emergency room at the local hospital with severe chest pains. I lay there sort of bouncing, on the gurney. I was twenty-nine. I was having a panic attack, but no one talked to me about that at the time, so I did not know what it was called. It wasn't until some months after remembering this that I realized what had caused my anxiety, or even that it was anxiety.

It was the week following Christmas 1975. We had travelled four and a half hours by car to celebrate Christmas with both our families. Following Christmas with my parents, we visited my aunty, where my parents, sister and I had lived for the first six and a half years of my life, while my parents built our home. My aunty had installed an in-ground pool, and we were delighted to allow our children to enjoy it. During the afternoon, my daughter, age three and a half, was rescued from drowning. Dan leapt in to pull her up by her arm as she stood on the bottom of the pool. She had jumped in to save her bigger brother, age five and a half, when she thought he was having trouble swimming. Neither of them knew how to swim.

My third child, age thirteen months, was unwell, and when we returned to my parents' home I wanted to settle him for the night. My father invited us to take all three children out to visit friends. Knowing these people very well, I knew my children would be expected to "be seen and not heard." I pointed out what I needed to do and declined to go.

My father was not happy with my refusal but even more so when he returned home later that night. With all three children safely asleep, I had joined the neighbour out on a picnic blanket in front of their house next door and shared a whisky. The day had been very hot and sultry, and we had waited in vain outside for the cooling southwest wind, called the Freemantle Doctor. My father's face was stormy and he stomped inside. When I went back inside my parents' house, and after a lot of angry words, he told me I was disinherited! I was no longer worthy of being in his will.

My sister had not taken her children visiting. I can only surmise that not having been discovered on the lawn with the neighbours, as she had gone inside, she did not deserve to be disinherited. She alone stood up for me, declaring to our father that he need not bequeath her anything either.

Twenty years later my mother rang distressed about that same couple. They had discovered the wife in tears when they went around to visit. She lifted the hem of her skirt to show severe bruising all up her legs where her husband had kicked her. My parents had never known that she was a battered wife throughout their decades of friendship. It was ironic that in the last year of his life, perhaps under the influence of steroids for his cancer, she rang complaining he had done the same thing to her.

I did not understand anything about cortisol or epinephrine or the fight/flight response. Perhaps dealing with a suspected heart attack a few days later was easier than addressing my father's rejection following the fear generated by my daughter's near drowning and a sick baby, all of which had led to a panic attack and my heart racing.

> Jen's Story
>
> Jen, in her sixties, happily married, adult children, had severe anxiety. Jen reported her husband laughing good-humouredly at her when she reported my suggestion she had fears of abandonment. He couldn't believe that she had only just worked that out. If he was just thirty seconds late, she would accuse him of forgetting her. He asked if she had told me about several incidents when as a young child her parents had accidentally not picked her up.
>
> Her husband waited decades for her to be ready to deal with her childhood and nurtured her during this time, so she felt worthy despite her fears. Her father had been a loving man, and earlier abandonment issues had occurred due to medical procedures, but they had not resulted in emotional estrangement. Her partner was similar to her father, thus ameliorating the situation for her.
>
> We successfully treated the anxiety with EMDR therapy by targeting the early trauma of the medical procedures and the episodes where she had accidentally been left on her own. The memories no longer triggered any emotional response. We next targeted present-day events to eliminate the emotional charge from those. After that, we explored and practised for future events. This resulted in reducing her overall level of anxiety and her general reactivity. This resulted in good control of her blood pressure and its effect on her heart, which was the initiating cause for her therapy.

When I was pregnant with my fifth baby, having attended a doctor's appointment, I arrived home from doing some casual work at the local high school. Dan was due home. The phone rang. It was a nurse from the Accident and Emergency department. "It's all right," she said. "I know you're pregnant, but your husband …" I knew he must have been alive, as he had told them I was pregnant. My doctor had told me to go home to rest, or else I was in danger of having the baby early. I had reassured both him and myself that as it was the last day of term, Dan would be able to look after me for the next two weeks as he had taken leave, and I would be able to take it easy!

I think this was the beginning of my growth into strength. Whereas a couple of years earlier I had been stressed to the point of thinking I was having a heart attack and I had been taken to the hospital with chest pains, now I was managing to be calm for the sake of the children and not needing to be calmed.

My father rang not many days later to inform me that my mother had had a radical mastectomy for breast cancer. She hadn't wanted me to worry, as I was pregnant and had gone into hospital for a biopsy, consenting to the mastectomy while she was anaesthetised if the biopsy was positive. With Dan resting in the backseat, I bundled the children and my very pregnant belly into the car and drove the four and a half hours to be with her.

Baby, of course, was duly born some ten days later, but as I noted before the nursing staff appeared more concerned for Daniel and his injuries, and when labour went into a halt, they sent him home. Admitted to the antenatal ward, it took some insistence from me in the middle of the night before they took me back to the labour ward, where the doctor on duty, apparently interested in getting home

> Debbie's Story
>
> Debbie, thirty-five, married, public servant, had three young children, worked full-time, complained that she had to do all the housework and child discipline. She had accepted this, as she had a core belief that she was not good enough. Living with her in-laws exacerbated the problems, as they had been opposed to the marriage, telling her she wasn't good enough for their son.
>
> Having dealt with the trauma she had suffered in childhood and the PTSD from a work injury, we addressed the current family situation. One means was to identify ways of teaching her children to take age-appropriate responsibility so leaving the house in the morning for school, childcare, and work went more smoothly.
>
> One issue was teaching the children to pick up their dirty clothes and put them in the linen basket to be washed. The problem was magnified by the fact that the father did not pick up his dirty clothes.
>
> With better self-esteem, now able to recognise that her needs mattered and there was no reason she should be picking up after her husband, Debbie discontinued washing anyone's clothes that were not put in the basket. Initially she had stated her husband could not help it as he "had been brought up that way." She discussed it with them all prior to beginning her campaign. It worked. He was not of the baby-boomer generation but from generation X (usually considered to be born between 1963 and 1980), often being the offspring of the early baby boomers. His attitude expecting his wife to be his servant in picking up after him was disrespectful.

before midnight, declared the baby was in distress and performed an emergency Caesarean section.

I later learned that he was renowned for intervening and saving mothers and babies—that he'd based the baby's distress on one instance of rapid heartbeat during a contraction. Such rapid increase in heart rate is a usual sign of a healthy reaction in a healthy baby to the momentary reduction in blood flow during a contraction of the uterus.

I again felt alone and unprotected. No one was there to prevent them from putting my legs in stirrups and not giving me time to birth my baby. Even my first baby had only been a five-hour labour. I needed someone on my side, but they hadn't even called Dan to tell him I had gone back into labour let alone required a Caesar.

We have a journey, each of us, lessons to learn. How to be weak and to grow strong again has been a lesson for me. How I gave away my power and gave away myself along with it is a lesson I am still studying. It has taken me sixty-seven years to begin to understand. I hope sharing part of my journey strengthens you too.

Daniel reassured me each time when I was pregnant that the baby would not be malformed, that I would love my babies. I had written that I was afraid my children would be crummy like some of the kids I taught and that I wouldn't love them. He told me any children I had would be lovely.

I was surprised when I did love them. I had no idea of the depth of love I would experience when I fell in love in those moments after birth. I did not fully comprehend the concepts of bonding and attachment that are now commonplace. It was right that my children were all born such beautiful little beings, and by my third child I came to expect that I would fall in love with them, so I developed greater trust in things going well.

However, during their childhoods, there were many times I could be concerned about the problems each one of my children displayed, so much that I was in danger of forgetting the many positives. I lay awake all night very concerned about my eldest son's development when he was not yet three. He had been hospitalized six months earlier and clung desperately to my skirt or slacks since that time. His speech development was poor as well. Even then, I was not that comforted by the assertion that Dan had been the same and my son would be okay.

I decided to stop focusing on what was wrong, or lacking, and see each child for the whole person each was, to stop focusing on the problems my children were having with reading or spelling or making friends. Rather, I began to trust that they were okay as they were and would continue being okay and that any challenges were things they could deal with and that my job was to help them deal with stuff, not prevent it, or worry that it would be insurmountable and life-destroying.

Beneath that anxiety was a fear that I could not cope on my own, was not good enough to cope on my own. I was anxious because I felt alone, due to lack of emotional support from my parents. I was insecure, as I could not rely on their assisting me with my emotions. They did not seem to appreciate I had any emotions, and they lacked any empathy for me.

After marriage, we had few holidays until retirement (when I took us on overseas trips), except for spending time with family when we travelled interstate to visit them. It was a long way across the Nullabor. After Dan became eligible for long service leave, we took the children out of school for the whole term, piled into our 1980 Volkswagen Bus, and spent months camping as we toured the centre of Australia and the eastern states. The older children became very adept at erecting the large family tent, eventually not needing any adult help. I had wanted to fulfil the obligations I had as president of the local CWL (Catholic Women's League). It seemed normal that my wishes were not important enough to delay plans until it would have suited me. It was as it had been with my parents, as they did not take into account my needs as a student when they took holidays.

Just prior to the formal separation, Daniel told me he had deliberately planned this camping trip, making me choose between being a mother and being president. A lifelong friend commented how aware she had been about how little I had wanted to go on this trip. Most people were amazed, as the eldest child was turning ten and the youngest, a breastfeeding toddler, still in nappies. I was extremely anxious about it, as we had plans to climb Uluru (Ayer's Rock), and I was terrified one of the children might fall. The previous year, a dingo had killed baby Azaria Chamberlain where we were to camp, and there were dingoes around that looked menacing.

Man as the Head of the Family, the Breadwinner

"As the church is subject to Christ, so let wives also be subject in everything to their husbands" (Ephesians 5).

My mother was willing to convert to Catholicism for my father, with the proviso that they would be "real Catholics," attending Mass every Sunday. Her offer was refused. My sister put her husband as head of the house, but as he was not religious, she willingly forwent her previous attachment to the Presbyterian Church, especially as several visits to the church included "fire and damnation" sermons that he found unwelcoming and punitive.

The Christian tenets so permeated the Australian culture to the point that they were obeyed even when that resulted in disaffection from its base. In the homogenous cultural milieu of the 1950s and '60s, the tenets of Christianity then were far more ubiquitous in Australia than now. Church attendance was higher, and laws reflected a strong power base that was a very conservative Christianity. The man was head of the household.

By the time I was nineteen, I had read the Bible completely three times using daily readings. This peaceful meditative activity was special to me, though I stopped this practice a few years after I married. I had no idea that the ordinary Catholic never read the Bible, and Dan rejected my attempts to share this activity. It is no wonder that I looked to my intended spouse to be the head of the household. I expected him to take the lead.

The third stage of moral development, as developed by Lawrence Kohlberg, is the "good girl" stage where, as is normal in moral development, I sought approval from others. This made me question how much my conversion to the Catholic faith was driven by still seeking to do whatever would gain others' approval. I had always strenuously denied I had changed my faith in order to marry him. I wondered if this was a case of "I protesteth too much"? Abiding by laws and doing one's duty is the next stage, and as I searched for answers, I saw that at the time of my marriage I had not completely grown past the need for reliance on someone else to guide my life choices.

I moved to the country to forget Dan. He offered to help by lending me money. I had no need for it. I was very good at organising my finances, having paid for my own car in the first year of teaching. Despite earning much same salary as me, Dan used his mother's car.

Seven weeks later, around the time we were engaged, I wrote to Daniel suggesting some things we needed to buy. However, I agreed when Daniel said it was unfair to do so until after we were married and we could choose together, so I didn't buy anything. Within a few months, I was commenting in my letters to him on the cookbooks, records, and furniture he had bought. The colour of an oak table was one item about which I wrote that didn't thrill me … "but black, really?" I was a little dismayed when twenty-four days before the wedding nothing had been done about the wedding rings, as there was no money to spare. I hope I didn't pay for them. He did write about needing to borrow money from his "wife" before we were actually married.

In letters to Dan, I asked how the mining company shares that he had purchased were going, hoped the wine wasn't being drunk without me, looked forward to listening to the records and reading the books he had bought, and enjoyed the discussion about the plots of the movies he had seen. I wasn't thrilled with his five pages of description of "Rosemary's Baby". I hoped to go on the next trip to some interstate sightseeing spot he wrote about and to enjoy future parties like the ones he described. I guess he spent his money on things other than the purchase of a car.

At the same time, I wrote I had not gone to a ball to which I had been invited, or out to dinner or to see a movie. I look at these letters now with different eyes. I tried to challenge the inherent disparity and the unfairness at the time, but I also unwittingly accommodated a view of compliance. I was very sensitive to any hint of disapproval and sought to avoid it.

At his instigation, I traded in my car for a larger one, as he wrote it would provide us with more fun than the washing machine I thought a priority. It was with some dismay I realised that from the time we married, he drove the car to work, dropping me off at my school, and after the baby was born, leaving me at home without one. It was many years before I again owned a car or had regular access to one.

My little 1968 Torana had delighted me. It gave me a great sense of independence. My mother bemoaned her loss of independence when she was not allowed to drive after her heart attack. I scolded her when I found out she had driven to the local shops before her doctor had given her the all-clear. Even then, thirteen years ago, I did not recognise how I had lost my independence when I surrendered my vehicle when I was married.

The unspoken but accepted tradition was that women only drove cars when a man was not available. This might have been challenged many years ago when I discovered my girlfriend's mother had always driven the family as her father never liked driving, but the fact was filed away and did not impact on my inability to consider the presumptions I had about women driving. It probably accounts for her not understanding why I didn't drive home from their place if we chose not to sleepover.

The week after I gained my driver's licence, to help my mother, I picked my father up from work. It was the only time I did as he pulled on the handbrake when I slowed at the corner of our street. He prided himself on his driving ability and loved the accolades he earned at work. He had not allowed me to learn to drive until I had purchased my own car and he never gave me a lesson or spent time in the car with me as I practised for the driving test. I had not been worthy of being taught by him how to drive.

It is with dismay I realise that I unconsciously emulated the same behaviour with my children. As well, I realise my attitude to my sons' desires to ride motorbikes reflected my father's attitude. I rationalised my opposition on safety grounds.

Dan gave me some driving lessons. Perhaps it dated from then but any suggestion that I should be a designated driver for an outing was rejected, as my driving skills were not admired. This echoed my father's attitude and I found it almost impossible to be assertive with regards to it. All the members of the family had totalled cars in accidents yet I was seen as less than sufficiently competent. In later years friends encouraged a sleepover after a dinner party, much to the amusement of our children. It never occurred to me to ring for a taxi. I was so pleased to see my children develop the habit of having a designated driver and I commented positively on how great it was if they caught a taxi home. Often with the women being pregnant or breastfeeding, the designated drivers were female!

I slowly surrendered step by step what little power I had in the relationship with Dan. As he wrote we didn't need two, I sold my tape recorder and agreed to stop "wasting" money buying the little gifts I posted to him. He also discovered I was not legally bound to contribute to a retirement fund after marriage. This had continual repercussions throughout my life on attitudes to superannuation savings.

Naomi's Story

Naomi complained that her husband made her write down every item on which she spent any money he allowed her, having co-opted money she had inherited and a superannuation payout. It had to tally with his accounting. He insisted on buying a new house she didn't want and prevented her from having lunch with friends or pursuing her passion for her hobby. He belittled his wife's ability to manage money even when she had demonstrated competence, as she had purchased her own car and an investment property before he came on the scene.

It had become "what is mine is mine and what is yours is mine too." He was operating as if it was the nineteenth century. She was now totally dependent financially on her husband. She displayed a great deal of bewilderment and resentment regarding these events.

There was a letter written to the school directorate concerning my request for a transfer back home after the wedding. It probably sounds quite impossible in the twenty-first century that a fiancé would actually write to her partner's employer without any suggestion it was authorised by me, the employee.

At the time, I did not recognise that these things marked the beginning of what people in the twenty-first century call financial bullying. In fact, the term would have held no resonance for me, even if I had heard it. Baby boomers[iv] were raised to believe the male was the "breadwinner," and it was up to his discretion how he spent his money. To a point, I accepted it, despite my frustrations. I hardly registered how my questioning went unheeded.

My father was laughed at for educating his daughters. His mates told him we would only get married. That, of course, was proof enough of the waste of educating my sister and me. While at university, I was delighted to hear that female teachers had won the right to equal pay. Until the 1950s, women in public service were required to resign as soon as they married as they were expected to be busy childbearing.

In Australia during the twentieth century, the use of the "male minimum wage"[14] underlined the role of the man as breadwinner, as it was set with the understanding that it provided enough income for a man to support his wife and children. I witnessed my aunt pressuring one of her sons to go to university because he would need good money to support his future wife and family. He went to university but never married or had children.

A husband exercising financial control was more of a norm in the '60s and '70s than it is now, though my peers have been astounded at my acceptance of this as they always had and expected an equal financial partnership. Until recently, I have heard advice given to women about learning to write a cheque and know how to pay bills in preparation for widowhood, as there was an assumption that older women may not know how to do such things.

Unaware of how money was handled within my parents' marriage, I never discussed it with anyone. The myth that I could not be trusted to spend within the budget prevailed for years, though recently a son stated that on the rare occasions when I did the shopping during his childhood, I "got the good stuff."

Housekeeping money was a different matter for most women than it was for me. The majority believed it was her right to have enough money for housekeeping and feeding and clothing the children. Thus, when a young tradesman in the 1970s decided not to give his wife housekeeping money one week, she retaliated. "That's okay, but I'll go down to your father now and tell him you've refused

[14] It was considered that women who worked obviously did not have anyone to support so were considered lucky to keep their wage for themselves. I knew this was not true as my aunt had divorced during World War Two and supported herself and my cousin. Despite doing the same work, women's salaries were often 60 to 80 per cent of their male counterparts.
The facts that showed working women were often supporting their families as lone parents took many years to effect a change, yet Australian women are still notoriously underpaid. In 1919, Justice Higgins set the first minimum wage for female workers in the clothing trades at 54 percent, as he considered this enough to support her through her own exertions.

to give me any money." This was fairly astute, as he worked for his father. The money was quickly placed on the table, and it never happened again. I never had money placed on the table. It never occurred to me to demand housekeeping money let alone spending money as he did all the shopping.

In my letters, I note I followed his economic advice and changed from using butter to the cheaper margarine, also choosing the brand he suggested. Months before the wedding, I wrote about changes in my cooking too, mentioning chilli con carne and a curry because he suggested they were economical.

There was a great desire to please that must have looked very submissive. In May 1969, I wrote: *How can I bear eighty-eight days* (before our wedding) *away from you if you're going to be cranky with me? … How I hate the idea that you are displeased with me. Does that sound medieval? … I want you to like what I do, and I hate doing things you don't like.*

Perhaps he read it as meaning I would not do anything he hated, but hopefully I wrote it meaning I did not want him to hate anything I did. More than that, I wanted him to like what I did. I had not intended not to do things I liked. I did not really believe there would be restrictions on shopping, dancing, or others things I enjoyed, like playing basketball or taking part in the local dramatics club, and I certainly couldn't imagine not having long conversations with other people. Yet he had told me that was what he expected.

After we had been engaged for a week, he wrote that he had considered what he wanted from me once we were married. He wanted me to be just like him, doing everything I did the way he would do it. I replied I was worried that it "makes me an appendage," and being known as Mrs. Daniel Heartley "is in complete ignorance of me." I preferred using my first name and his surname. *It still lets me be me. I don't want to lose my identity.* This seems very antiquated now. I was worried about *childbearing being a completely fulltime job* and asked for his help to do other things, like write and study or tutor. I did not want to *become boring* but to have *something to talk about besides babies and nappies.*

He replied with best wishes for my role in the dramatic stage production that weekend, telling me to do my best, having stated I was half of him and so needed to do my best for him. I never participated in another dramatic production in my life. Looking at this exchange now, I realise it was the pattern for our communication. The salient point of the communication was not addressed. I wanted to talk about something as important as my being an individual. I became frustrated when a minor point became the focus of the conversation and the main point was ignored.

When I said I did not like something, like in the 1990s I refused even to look at an expensive beige leather lounge suite, my opinion was not important and the suite was duly delivered with the explanation that it had been on sale and too good an opportunity to miss. I hated that lounge! All my points about it needing a lot of work to keep it clean, or being sticky in summer and cold in winter were deemed irrelevant.

The week before the wedding, he wrote telling me we had to give up many things to be together, noting there would be little communication with others and that I would not have the freedom I had. He wrote how important this was to him and hoped I would not think he was being selfish. Rereading it, I noted that any surrender seemed to be on my side, not his. He concluded with commenting on how he felt so much better after writing it. I was glad he was feeling better, because even back then I wasn't.

Prior to the lovely ubiquitous mobile phone of today, rapid communication was via telegram. Not everyone in Australia in the late 1960s had a telephone connected, especially when they lived in rented premises. On one occasion I did not send a telegram stating I had arrived back home. On May 22, 1969, I wrote an apology: "I am terribly sorry about the telegram. Please forgive me. You sound so unhappy, and I didn't want to make you unhappy—it was terribly inconsiderate of me, and I don't want to be inconsiderate: …

'homecoming'? How can it be when the only home I can have is with you? You put such bitterness in your letter, as though I had done something to hurt you." Confusingly, nearly two months earlier I had promised I would not send telegrams, because he didn't like them.

I did not comprehend the huge future financial restrictions, nor did I understand how there could be the social isolation he anticipated with pleasure, as he wrote he wanted to be communicating with me without outside influences. I could not see how that was possible. I had friends, family, work colleagues, and neighbours and thought he was being romantic, wanting to be close. I was naïve.

I knew I was expected to love him so he wouldn't be unhappy, to look after myself for him, and to make his happiness my responsibility. I held some reservations, expecting us both to learn to control our moods after we married. I agreed about the need to establish trust for love to grow, that we needed to communicate our feelings. With only five weeks until the wedding, I was writing asking for his understanding, hoping he loved me and wanted him to write to me too. I asked him not to be bossy or supercilious but to be warm toward me.

I desperately sought approval. Dan had taken photos at my sister's wedding and wrote that I had spoiled them. I apologised profusely. I wrote back to Dan stating I hoped I wouldn't spoil our wedding photos. My need for his approval created great anxiety for me.

Sexuality

Within twelve months, he broke off our relationship for the first time. The reason he gave was that I was not a virgin, and he added I was leading him astray. In the sixties, being sexually active was unacceptable and any girl who was not a virgin was considered "damaged goods." With poor skin, wearing spectacles, shy, thinking

I was not as good as he academically with no other boys asking me out, I accepted his assessment of me. I was not good enough.

The look on his face was one that would become familiar to me. There was no movement in his features; his voice was calm and his eyes unblinking. As a therapist, I would now describe him as having a flat affect. I did not comprehend what was happening. My mind went blank and I couldn't speak.

This was the communication style I never understood throughout the relationship, but on reflection I realise it very effectively shut down most opposition from me. He was very proud of his ability to control decisions in this manner. He used it to great advantage at work. An executive meeting discussed shutting down his research program. When asked his opinion at the end of two hours he quickly gave an assessment that was irrefutable and so saved the project. I asked him why he did not say so immediately. He stated everyone had to express their feelings and if he made his statement before they had stated how they felt its impact would be lost. I took a long time to realise there did not need to be a meeting of more than two for this ploy to work. I would be so focused on the emotional part of a statement that I would let the rest slip by.

Not being a virgin was the shaming focusing factor. His proposition that it was my fault that he was sexually involved with me and no longer a virgin himself distracted me. I did not respond with a vehement admonition to him that he had to take responsibility for his own sexual involvement. I did not appreciate that he saw women the way the church did at that time. A woman had to be a virgin, a Madonna or a whore. I was shocked when he said forty-six years later that I had taught him sex was dirty. This attitude made bookends to the relationship that had lasted my entire adult life.

His ambivalence around sex coloured our relationship in what I now view as a very unhealthy manner. Funny the way dates recur through one's history. Thirty years earlier to the day of my daughter's second marriage, Dan had written to me about the importance of physical contact for love to grow. Just prior to our engagement, he wrote he believed that men who stayed away from their wives, who did not touch them or listen to them or see them, caused their own marriages to break down. He attributed this to the fact that people lose their sense of togetherness when they stop thinking of each other as a person.

Months later, I wrote, asking him to "Please … don't feel love play is a waste of time. After all, that is what tells me you love me." Two days earlier I had also written, apologising: "I stir you sexually and not emotionally." I reassured him that making love when your basic desire is satisfaction … "is supposed to be normal. It just seems awful because at the moment it isn't in a complete perspective of usual loving times—we try to squash all our loving into a little time and it comes out a bit distorted."

I realise now that I had a limited understanding about the role sexual intimacy can play in a relationship. A day earlier I had written concerning communicating with each other, how when one of us made a gesture toward the other it was necessary to respond in kind—such as a kiss in return, not an angry word.

I apologised for being sexually attractive while being inadequate in inspiring his affection. I thought that after we were married there would be no problem with our sex life, though I had serious concerns about family planning. In his letters were numerous comments and encouragement to me about going to confession. He expressed great concern that feelings of guilt might result in a hating of the sex act, which he wrote caused him confusion as to whether he loved me or not.

When considering whether or not to request an early transfer back home months prior to the wedding, Dan wrote how stressful my friends had found preparing for their wedding and at the same time how difficult abstaining from sex had been for them. He advised against the request. I never asked my girlfriend about this until after I reread about it in our correspondence. She was staggered and had no memory of there being any distress or reporting any such distress to anyone.

One thing I never asked him about was when he wrote discussing whether someone allowing another to quench his sexual desires would affect his relationship with his wife. I guess I didn't want to know the answer.

Family Planning

In the pre-marriage correspondence, I wrote pages about my desire to spend some time as a couple before having children. "Is it wrong that we should want each other's body for joyful intimacy, without children? I feel that to conceive a child soon would interfere with the initial growth of our marriage." He, however, believed that Pope Paul VI's encyclical, *Humanae Vitae*, released in 1968, forbade use of any contraceptive and used many arguments to sway me.

I had been prescribed an oral contraceptive for other health reasons, but I did not use the prescription I had, for my first child was born nine months after I returned from my honeymoon, so he obviously won me over to his way of thinking. One argument Dan used was that I was obviously not very fertile, as infrequent lovemaking before marriage had not resulted in a pregnancy.

He told me he had visited the priests, where he had taken me to that first Mass in 1966, to discuss "my" problem, being my desire to use the oral contraceptive for health reasons, even though I knew it would also prevent conception. I realise now that he was using what is called referent authority to endorse his position. Having had a very emotional experience there (I often mentioned how special going to Mass there was for me), he used my feelings for that place and the priests to add power to his arguments.

I also greatly admired my future in-laws, and their acceptance of babies was a very different cry from the rejection my mother expressed. She had been horrified when she saw me knitting baby clothes for his mother! She firmly believed babies should be born before a woman was thirty to ensure they were not left motherless at a young age like she was. When I converted to Catholicism, I was warned by her not to arrive back home with six kids. I remember being terrified when I rang to inform her of my later pregnancies. She was not the only one to express distaste for a large family. I was more than mortified when a female workmate of Dan's had visited me after the birth of my youngest child and had literally flung a gift onto the bed stating how little she agreed with my having had another baby.

Without any medical problem necessitating any such intervention, after the birth of my third child, my obstetrician offered to do a tubal ligation then and there, as I was "open" and it wouldn't even need an anaesthetic! It had not been discussed in any antenatal visit and I found it very distressing to be so importuned moments after giving birth. I doubted the ethical integrity of a doctor behaving in this way and chose to see general practitioners for subsequent births.

I never gave voice to my concerns possibly because one group of people including my family and friends would have totally endorsed the obstetrician's viewpoint while the other group of in-laws and church would have not understood why it even bothered me. I can't remember if I talked with Dan about it, but I assume I didn't since he would have not understood how it made me feel.

The greatest referent power Dan borrowed was from the pope, though I was ambivalent about this. In his *Humanae Vitae*, Pope Paul VI endorsed use of the Billings method of detecting ovulation,[15] which I learned when I was pregnant with my second child. During our courtship, I had worried about withholding our love on occasion because, as I wrote, "I wouldn't be able to turn away. I fear you would leave it up to me. Please don't make me responsible."

However, it always was my responsibility as I was the only one who wanted to plan our family. There was never any clarity about how many children we would have, and I found him wanting as

[15] The Billings method of detecting ovulation was/is taught to women. The official website states that The Billings Ovulation Method is used by millions of women around the world. This implies women are responsible for its use. http://www.thebillingsovulationmethod.org/.

many children as came along a very scary prospect. I never had the conviction or depth of faith that this was right, perhaps because my beliefs were not rooted in a Catholic upbringing. My plans were truncated to what I could complete in less than nine months, as I had a continuous fear of another pregnancy. I undertook my postgraduate studies with a new baby having calculated I could complete them, as lactation would delay ovulation for at least a year.

In my early forties, I did resort to a tubal ligation as a permanent solution. Dan no longer urged me to have more pregnancies because of what the church stated, but using the referent authority again of his mother and aunts, he did refer to how happy they all were, having had children later in life. At the end of the marriage, he told me he had wanted eight children. Unsurprisingly, this was one more than his father. It was a competition I never would have entered!

At the end of the marriage, I realised that every time I had wanted to discuss the very important issue of how many children we should or could have, my concerns were, as in every other area, bypassed for his then unspoken preference of having more children. I asked him then why, if he actually loved me, he didn't ever ask how many children I wanted. It dismayed me that I had never thought to ask this during the marriage.

His answer then was that he knew how I had felt, so he did not need to ask me. With his flat affect and monotone voice, he stated, "You always felt physically uncomfortable, bloated, hated having morning sickness, disliked the burping, indigestion, flatulence, the baby hiccoughing and squirming and you hated being tired and were very emotional. I put up with that so I could have another baby." I knew Dan thought I was his cross to bear, something that, when he said it on many occasions, made me feel less than worthy. This was an instance of what he believed he had to tolerate. It did not display any empathy for me.

Pope Paul VI stated periodic abstinence would allow couples to develop their personalities and promote kindness and love for each other. His Holiness asserted that contraception by contrast reduced a woman to a tool for a man's satisfaction of his desires and that he would cease to show care and affection to his wife.

Over the years, I found what I learned with the Billings Method did not prepare me for the indignity of being a woman wanting to make love around oestrus,[16] when the libido is heightened. I resorted on occasion to sleeping at the end of the bed to prevent touching, but I never discussed this with anyone as I was too embarrassed.

I not only used the Billings Method but also was actively involved in teaching it. Perhaps now they teach about the many different ways of expressing emotions and love through communication, touch, hugs, acts of service, and gifts so abstinence does not become so intolerable. The irony is that the Billings Method resulted in the very problems for me that the other contraceptive methods His Holiness condemned were predicted to do. However, I don't believe the method was responsible for the problems but masked what was already there and had been from the very beginning of the relationship.

Although Pope Paul VI noted that coercing sex was not an act of love, I cannot find any reference in his encyclical that the denial of lovemaking could be a denial of love, as he assumes that a couple will show love and kindness in other ways.

"The husband should give to his wife her conjugal rights, and likewise the wife to her husband. For the wife does not rule over her own body, but the husband does; likewise the husband does not rule over his own body, but the wife does. Do not refuse one another except perhaps by agreement for a season, that you may devote yourselves to prayer; but then come together again, lest Satan tempt you through lack of self-control" (1 Corinthians 7:3–5).

Working It Through

How closely do your partners resemble a parent?

---

[16] See http://www.ncbi.nlm.nih.gov/pmc/articles/PMC2394562/ for discussion of why oestrus is applicable to humans.

I have heard many say they married their father, or their mother. However, perhaps for you, as for me, the list resembled a list of opposites.

Write the three attributes of your opposite-sex parent that most distressed you in your childhood. Include as many physical attributes, personality characteristics, talents, achievements, attitudes, and anecdotes as you can, as it will help you identify the similarities and differences, both of which are important.

1.
2.
3.

Compare with your partners past and present. Are these the same attributes of your partner that are the most problematic?

Opposite-Sex Parent

On the other hand, clients have told me their same-sex parent was more influential in their choice of partner. My mother was absent, unambitious, and never talked to me about emotions.

Again I find that these initially were traits whose opposite I pursued. I wanted someone who would spend time with me, who displayed some ambition to learn and create a career and interesting life, and who talked about how he felt. Yet as with my father's traits, the superficial understanding I had of these traits misled me.

Write the three attributes of your same sex parent that most distressed you in your childhood.

1.
2.
3.

Some Special Issues

Sex

1. Is sexual intimacy something you share?
2. Are you equal partners?
3. Do you both have the same right to initiate sex play?
4. Is it fun?
5. Do you give the same respect to the other in accepting a "Not tonight, Josephine"?
6. Do you often seek not to be close?
7. Do you both feel comfortable about asking for what your body and soul crave during this physical closeness?
8. Are each of you heard?
9. Are you patient, kind, and gentle with each other?
10. Is there always an agenda for one of you other than loving each other, whether it is making babies, climaxing, or an outlet for tension and being able to relax?
11. Do you feel closer or more distant after making love?
12. Has it changed since you married or made a commitment to each other?
13. Has it changed since retirement, or any other event in your life: first, last baby, a trauma, a bereavement, a life-challenging event or since turning a certain age?
14. What are you aware of concerning the sexual intimacy of your parents and your partners' parents?
15. Are you both content with the frequency of sexual intimacy?

Family Planning

1. Have you discussed whether you want to have children?
2. Do you feel comfortable talking about this?
3. Does your partner feel comfortable talking about this?

4. How do you know what your partner is thinking and feeling about this?
5. How many children do you want?
6. How many children does you partner want?
7. How are you going to achieve family planning?
8. Whose responsibility is contraception?

The woman sat in my office in tears. "There's training twice a week, and then a game on the weekend, but this also includes watching other games, not just playing his own, plus following it on television and going interstate to watch away games. It dominates our lives, yet he won't give me what I passionately want." Her partner expected her life to revolve around his interests and would not countenance another baby. What do you think about this?

Another thirty-one-year-old woman was worried about her biological clock ticking and wanted to have a child. However, her partner said he was not interested at the moment but to ask him in five years. What do you think about this?

I am not the only woman to not really hear what her boyfriend was saying. A classmate at my fiftieth reunion reported her husband has said he never wanted children or a white picket fence. After seven years, when he had them both, they divorced. I did not really hear how much my partner wanted a very large family.

How common is it, do you think, that we don't hear what our partner is saying?

Financial Matters

1. Are you comfortable talking about money?
2. If not, do you know why?
3. Do you need to do some research to help?
4. Should you have a budget?
5. Do you have financial goals?

6. Should partners make the same contribution in absolute terms or as a percentage of their income?
7. Should partners share the same account? Why?
8. How regularly should you discuss finances? Why?

Social Life

1. Do you agree on your holidays and their frequency, location, and style?
2. Do you agree on social activities?
3. Do you maintain individual friends, activities, and/or hobbies?

From my journal, June 27, 1969

Alone Again
As darkness creeps to blanket my bed
loneliness wraps me in its shroud
and all warmth leaves me. Cold I lie,
impatient for the sun that brings
me breath. So I watch the stars
that were delighted conspirators in our game,
but now they blink, lest
they see where once was life,
a nothing.

Chapter 7

ON THE EDGE OF MY LIFE

It was Sunday. The day was sunny and warm, and as my children and their families arrived, they were excited about the prospect of a swim in the pool. The tables in the summerhouse were set. As others arrived, the noise gradually increased to its usual volume. It was not the first time that I wondered if squealing children and raucous men might have irritated my neighbours. I thought of the house where my children grew up. The neighbours had become close friends, and we shared many a Sunday afternoon.

As wine and beer were consumed, the voices of the drinkers rose in volume, mostly in good-hearted debate about the state of the Australian cricket team or some work-related issue. Most of the women were focused on their toddlers, feeding them, changing clothes, and taking them for a swim in the pool. The older children exuberantly jumped in the pool and played games.

One little grandson wanted me to play with him. He loved the collection of colourful boxes brought home from Egypt, Holland, Belize, Brazil, Spain, England, Russia, Malaysia, Philippines, China, Italy, Singapore, Germany, Sweden, Switzerland and Vietnam. He carefully placed boxes inside each other, sorting them out as to what fit where, and it seemed to me that I was doing the same thing with my life. As we sat on the carpet, even though I engaged with him, fetching boxes from the cabinet, assisting him where needed, encouraging him to try different arrangements, I felt some detachment from him as I kept being drawn back to those letters from the 1960s and my younger self. She seemed so real to me. She had never been away. It was like she was screaming, why didn't you listen to me?

Perhaps because I had lost so much weight I recalled what it was like when I was younger and weighed the same. I have this lovely photo of me in 1989. I am slender and full of energy. Teachers where I worked were surprised I was old enough to have a son at university.

A bush dance was held that year at the parish hall. We had sat at dinner with neighbours and close friends from the parish, including my youngest son's godparents, who had given me a surprise fortieth birthday party. They were people with whom we frequently had barbeques in each other's backyards. The only person Daniel had spoken to all night was me, and as we were swirling around on the dance floor and I was having a great time, he said, "I'm bored." I have been crushed ever since. Even after twenty years, I was still not enough: not pretty enough, not slim enough, not smart enough, not interesting enough.

No wonder I began to pad myself up after that. During the day he had emailed me a previous year's holiday photo of us dancing. I was enjoying myself then too. He spoiled it when he sat down and stated how lucky I had been as he gave me two dances and he had only intended one. He commented in the email I had lost my big shoulders now. It seemed, like the boxes my little grandson was playing with, each memory had another nested within it.

My youngest grandson joined us. His favourite choice was the nested Russian babushka dolls. I attempted to focus on his delight and helped him place the correct doll within the next size, but my mind wandered. On Saturday, the day before, when I returned happy with a sense of accomplishment from my walk, Dan had greeted me with stories about women who have been abducted when out walking, stuffed into trunks of cars, raped, and murdered.

One of my sons walked through to the bathroom to shower. It reminded me how the previous week, when I had my hair done and felt contented the way any woman does after a visit to her hairdresser, Dan peered at me, looking hard, walking around me a bit and turned on the light, declaring he couldn't see what they had done. My son had complimented me that night at dinner with, "Your hair looks good, Mum."

That Sunday I did not know how to I interpret this. I did not have time to wonder about the function of the negative comments. I was acting as an observer to my life. I had been raised to comply with my husband's wishes far more than I thought. However, like many female baby boomers, I was less submissive after a few decades of some independence of thought, action, and finances achieved through following a career.

Everyone lined up with plates at the barbeque. I took the large casserole dishes of baked summer vegetables out to the tables as the meats were served. Salads and breads were already out. People rearranged seating as suited them, and children were quickly towelled dry, with a promise of a later swim to the older ones. The younger preschoolers had all been bathed and dressed.

Dan was standing up, drinking a glass of wine. He was cajoled to sit down to eat by a grandchild. Plans for our upcoming holiday were discussed. After eating, beginning to clear the tables, I collected a lot of bottles and cans in my arms and took them out the front to the recycling bin. It usually took some six trips to clear them all away.

Turning back to go inside, I tripped over a fitting for the back of the caravan parked near the bins. The sensor light had been turned off, and in the dark, I had misjudged where the equipment was. I walked a little stiffly through the front door to examine the damage and then cleaned off the blood that was oozing from several cuts on my knee and shins.

Some of the family noticed me sitting on a couch, my legs elevated with an icepack, and showed some concern. My eldest was furious when he discovered the sensor light had been switched off to save electricity. However, they all duly left, and Dan stood in the open front door wanting me to come outside so he could show me how to walk along the front of the house without falling over. I refused. I was too embarrassed to go out in case the neighbours saw us.

There was no sitting together and chatting about the evening, filling in information or anecdotes about what the family were doing. He took himself off to bed as soon as everyone had gone. While I spent several hours clearing tables to stack and clear the dishwasher, though some assistance had been given by family before they carted tired children home, I had plenty of time to think. The next day there was washing and ironing of tablecloths and napkins, washing, drying, and folding twenty beach towels, rearranging furniture, clearing away rubbish, including the cigarette butts from my daughter's smoking, and more thinking time.

This was not what I wanted in retirement for the next twenty years. I skimmed the surface, thinking I didn't want to sit at home knitting, doing crafts, planning holidays, doing Sudoku or crosswords or cross-stitch, or spend endless hours gardening, caring for chooks or a vegetable patch. I had already tried to do that and it did not satisfy me, despite the activities being ones I enjoyed. I recalled many years ago Anne, a kindergarten teacher, returned to work after retirement. She explained to me that she gained far more from her teaching than she did "holding things" for her retired husband or making endless cups of tea when he demanded.

In the following weeks, my thoughts turned to other women and retirement. My girlfriend thought of these years as her golden years, but it wasn't a universal sentiment. My favourite dress shop assistant, age sixty-two, declared she would be at the shop early on Anzac Day, otherwise she would have to be at home with her husband. Three women at the small community markets commented that their craftwork of knitting, sewing, or crocheting kept them off the streets and out of trouble and pleased their husbands.

Over the years, our lives had become very restricted socially, with visits to friends and family and only ever as a couple or a family. Where once we had attended parties, wine tastings, and lectures, and studied together, he was saying he did not want to leave the house as he had everything there he wanted. I didn't.

Occasional dinners and theatre outings or visits to the movies occurred after the first twenty years, but when all the children had left home and partnered, I thought I could go for lunch like other women did: meeting my friends for coffee, going with my friends for dinner, lingering if I liked somewhere, seeing a movie, or even taking a longer-than-usual walk. My arriving home later than he expected, his sarcastic comments saying he was about to call the police quickly reinforced the belief that it was still not okay, as it had not been in 1969 when I did not send a telegram to say I had arrived. It was reminiscent of this earlier behaviour. Although decades late, I had begun to assert my right to a life.

One of the things that had irritated me about my first fiancé was that he did not want to do things with me. We had planned to construct an elaborate fish aquarium and bought the tank and all the paraphernalia. I was so disappointed when I arrived at his place to be greeted with, "Look what I did for you." At nineteen, I did not have a name for what he was doing, but he was being manipulative and controlling and I rejected it. These many years later, I realised I only rejected it then because it was at such variance with what I wanted to do. I had not recognised the essence of it as controlling. When things were closer to my own goals, I did not recognise the manipulation, but I was doing so now.

Later that week, in recliner chairs like Mama bear and Papa bear, his chair slightly bigger than mine, I sat watching a movie he had chosen. I was very aware of Dan but was paralysed, unable to speak or turn toward him, as Meryl Streep attempted to coax life back into marriage with Tommy Lee Jones in *Hope Springs*. In her negligee, she leaned against the architrave in the doorway of his separate bedroom only to be refused entry or interest.

I was devastated that I could be in a room beside the man I had devoted my life to for forty-six years and be so uncomfortable that I could not speak about the theme of a romance movie. It mirrored my experience too closely. "Are you looking for some testosterone?" I had been asked when I had attempted to initiate sex not many nights before.

By the end of the movie, my stomach was in knots, my throat so constricted I found it hard to swallow. However, I took the opportunity to suggest we could do some marriage counselling but was told it would be pointless. "You are not interested in changing", he said. I was told I was happy as I was doing what I wanted to do. I spent the night in tears while he slept on the far side of the king-sized bed.

I never expected to be lonely once married. It was the times during courtship when there was no certainty about the relationship in which loneliness loomed as a spectre. For twenty-five years, the physical closeness of raising children had sustained me. It seemed the only time we had anything to talk about now was when we travelled. Over the past ten years, I had planned many long trips. When questioned about not retiring, I pointed out the value of my extra income paying for overseas travel.

I thought about our lack of conversation and touch. Rather than book a quiet dinner for the two of us to celebrate his birthday some months earlier, I spent nearly a thousand dollars on taking the whole family out to dinner at a restaurant, ostensibly as a surprise. Otherwise we would have sat there with nothing to share. There would have been no handholding, or even a touch of a hand on my back guiding me into the restaurant. Indeed, when he saw everyone there already seated, he was several paces in front of me and engaged in handshaking and conversation before I had gone beyond the foyer.

What had happened? Had endless "admin" meetings about who was to take which child where and when or what furniture to buy or where to live, to what country to travel, what money to put in what investment, or what piece of furniture needed revamping murdered intimacy? Attempting to identify what was missing, I realised that even if intimacy meant more than conversation and physical touch, I was now missing out on even those basic things.

I pictured being at ease with him, touching him, talking about the exciting things we were doing, seeing, planning, and sharing for the last quarter of our lives. I had been insulted when he put a question mark after the word *love* on an anniversary card for our thirty-eighth wedding anniversary. Five years later, things had deteriorated even further.

Movies became a window into my heart. Kate Winslet's character in the film *The Holiday* is told by Eli Wallach's character, Arthur, a long-forgotten famous film scriptwriter, that there are two roles: the leading lady and the best friend. Kate immediately recognised that she should definitely be the leading lady in her own life.

I knew I had become one of the aunts at the wedding, that the bright young things were served before me at the shop counter, and I didn't quite count, and that somehow I had been relegated to a supporting role.

How did this happen?

It had been a slow process. I thought about the first time I had felt sidelined. I was at my daughter's twenty-first birthday party. She was married, so she gave herself the celebration in her own home. I was a guest, not the hostess. It was a weird sensation. Perhaps another woman would have put on an apron and bustled about, preparing, serving, clearing away, and maintained a semblance of importance, of usefulness, within her own eyes. However, my daughter was well schooled in how to be a hostess, and there was little to do but admire her as she catered to her guests and looked after the needs of her partner and my little granddaughter.

I mingled and chatted with family and her friends, but on the edge. Although it was more than twenty years ago, I still felt that fuzziness in my head, the slump of my shoulders, the tension in my jaw as I sat in her dining room, wondering what I was supposed to do. One young guest cornered me to discuss his depression.

Perhaps six years earlier was the first glimpse I had that I didn't quite register, watching my eldest son bend over and kiss his girl good-bye after I had picked them up from a school dance. I was taken aback at how grown up he was. A recent experience of being told to age gracefully was at my youngest son's wedding, when another son, flattering my younger sister, suggested I too should let my hair remain grey. "You should age gracefully, Mum, like your sister."

Old, elderly, aged, gone.

I asked myself if it was simply a generational change. Was it simply a new generation asserting itself? Was it a matter of how very different the new generation was from mine? Was I feeling jealous as I was pushed aside by generation X?

I was quite annoyed by the media depiction of older people. In a newspaper, a seventy-three-year-old male victim of a bashing is described as *elderly.* Even worse, on the television, I was furious that a couple who were victims of a home invasion were described as an "elderly" couple—he was sixty-three and she fifty-eight! I have complained to friends that if I were the subject of a story, a journalist would gleefully describe me as a great-grandmother.

The term conjured an image for me of a frail, slightly bent over figure, unable to walk far, shuffling along, in my late eighties, with sparse, thin grey hair, fingers clawed with arthritis, with a croaky failing voice. Well, I don't look like that at all. My mythical journalist might want to evoke sympathy for me as a very defenceless, extremely old, weak woman, to encourage readers to have greater empathy for me or to whip up anger against the perpetrator. However, I resent this as it plays into the hands of society to marginalise older women. My value is not enhanced but reduced to that of an ancestor, as something valued by the potential importance of the life of someone much younger. It is part of the continuation of pressure on women to conform to their biological status as child-bearers.

It was a hot Australian Christmas day. I opened the gift from my in-laws. My father-in-law sat smiling at me. My young teenage brothers-in-law were present, along with a sister-in-law and my mother-in-law. There were a few of their little grandchildren too, including two of my children crowded into the small lounge room, dominated by a large Christmas tree. I pulled out a diaphanous black negligee set. My eyes darted back and forth, as I didn't know what to say. My father-in-law said, "I got that for you. I want another grandchild." I felt humiliated but laughed it off, pretending it was unimportant.

Three decades later, Daniel frequently questioned a daughter-in-law about when she was going to have a baby. When she did have a baby, he then asked her when the second baby was to be expected. He didn't bother with gifts the way his father had, though he was extremely pleased when he was able to go into the garage that was packed with an extra of this or that and give her an iron when she said she needed to buy one. He continued the line that as many babies that came along was the way to plan a family. Unwittingly, I may have exerted pressure on her too by standing there quietly as if assenting to it. I was not yet aware of what I felt.

I noticed that when older women met, the small-talk included, "And how many grandchildren do you have?" They often volunteered their score. Producing grandchildren had become a competition, one I never volunteered to enter but very rarely lost. Yet it is a strange competition: copulation and birthing decades earlier, and the decision whether or not further input was required was not under my control. When I saw my first grandchild, but hours old, I realised with a pang in my heart that I could only love her with the permission of her mother. I was reassured for many years, as she never seemed to place restrictions on how I loved her children.

When my first child was five months old, I returned to teaching. Both his grandmothers minded him over the next five months. I missed him terribly and resigned, aware I was jealous of their days with him, afraid I was missing out on his development and love.

Fortunately, I surrendered these feelings, and he and his siblings had the blessing of some long-lived grandparents and have been able to nurture their relationships with them.

I did not have long-lived grandmothers. My paternal one had died when I was seven and the maternal one long before I was born. I have no memory of my maternal grandfather, and those of my pop are of a huge man who struggled up the driveway having removed two walking sticks from the sidecar of a motorbike he had dismounted, or of a grisly, rough, bewhiskered kiss that scraped my face.

I was never left with my grandparents. They never looked after me while my parents went out or on holiday. They did not pick me up from school. Even though I was left alone after school with my sister from the age of nine, I never heard any discussion about having us supervised. No grandparent played games with me or read a book. They never taught me anything. My nana gave me a fine china set of a cup, saucer, and plate as a start for my glory box in preparation for my marriage. I was six or seven.

My mother approached being a grandmother the same way she approached motherhood. She interpreted nurturing in the same fashion as providing care and food and entertainment. She did not have a career, even though she had been employed outside the home. Like most of her generation, my mother did not have grandparents on which to model her behaviour any differently.

My children reproduced, and they, along with society, expected me as a mature woman to fulfil a very traditional, nurturing role. I assisted my daughter and her daughter to complete their education that had been interrupted by teen pregnancies, through babysitting so they could attend classes. It was not an accident that every shopping mall around the country was full of strollers being pushed by other grandparents. At every school I visited to pick up grandchildren, a myriad of other grandparents were doing likewise.

I had to be very clear with my children about how I loved their children but did not want to raise them. This clarity, however, took nearly twenty years to evolve! I refused to babysit so mothers could return to their careers. Having babysat older grandchildren, there was pressure that somehow I owed the same level of service to others, but I did not. I had babysat so girls could be educated and have decent jobs. I was not going to retire from a career I loved to assist others to have theirs when I had sacrificed twelve years to raising my own children. It was patently unjust. The problem for me was I always accepted the subtle impositions, and it had to be fairly blatant for me to resist.

It reminded me of the issue of living in a caravan. Dan had wanted us to save money by living in a caravan for the first three years of our marriage. I said a resounding no to that, but when it came to living on the same side of town as my best friend, with two children younger than four and pregnant, I could not muster enough energy to win. Isolating me from outside influences had been a continuous activity, the import of which eluded me until after I left the marriage. I then realised that each house move had reduced my social network so that eventually I did not have any friends amongst my neighbours or in the new church parish, as any social contact with them when I suggested it was refused.

Babysitting turned into childminding when the child could not cope with too much regimented after-school care or he or she missed me and preferred to be with me. When I demurred, there was the threat that if I did not want a relationship with my grandchildren then that was okay, they would not be brought around. I ignored the threat at the time, though I was aware of the emotional manipulation that motivated it.

Yet from the look of the parks and playgrounds, a lot of us haven't been able to do this or have acceded to it. Some embrace it wholeheartedly, perhaps even believing they are better than their children at raising children. No paradox there, I trust. Others told me they had wished they'd had some such help, and having not received it, gave it to vicariously satisfy their own needs.

Many women have found themselves seemingly locked into years of unpaid, unappreciated childminding. One of my cousins spent eight years travelling forty minutes each way to and fro from her child's home, virtually raising her grandchildren. Another woman told me her grandchild was dropped off with dirty nappies and expected to be clean and happy ten hours later when he was picked up as his mother raced back from the gym or shopping after work before tearing off home for dinner. Scarcely a word would be spoken.

Sometimes I initiated the question about grandparent status. It is a habit I am trying to break. I was staggered when one friend revealed that she had been a grandmother for half a dozen years before she found out. Involvement with the grandchildren ranged from total estrangement to enmeshment so intense that the grandparent was raising the grandchildren. Grandmothers revealed a great deal of emotional pain when they had never seen, rarely saw, or no longer saw their grandchild. Others revelled in frequent visits, saw childminding as a privilege, or were delighted in taking the grandchild on holidays. However, for as many as took delight in these activities, there were those who found this a burden.

Another part of the competition I participated in was the "naming." It is the "What are you going to be called?" question. Some opt out of this, to varying degrees, beginning by refusing to be called anything vaguely like Nana or Grandma, Pop, Pa, or Granddad. Some of my cousins called my grandfather Adi, though he was "Pop" to me. Here in Australia, some choose Gros Papa, or Oma, Dedo, or Bubba from other cultures, not necessarily because of a family cultural connection but because they like the sound of it.

Then they may be called by a variation of their given names, like the fabulous grandmother of my childhood neighbour. How I longed to have an "Amanda Francis" who swept up the driveway next door to my childhood home in a full cloak, bearing armfuls of gifts bought in exotic places. I didn't realise for many years that she was a grandmother. I tried to bring that sense of the exotic into the way I developed my role as a grandmother, taking delight in providing a granddaughter with dolls from faraway places and a grandson with models of iconic buildings he collected.

With my turn to choose a name, my first names didn't seem at all exciting the way hers had. Some go for variations, cutely choosing derivations of their names by doubling the first syllable, but doubling some names would be gross and thankfully did not occur to me or anyone else!

I have been groomed my whole life for grandparenting and old age. I use the term *groomed* purposefully. The dictionary defines grooming as preparing a person for a particular position or purpose. I have become sickeningly familiar with the concept of grooming of children by paedophiles for sexual exploitation. I have witnessed the devastating results in schools and in my office every year. Those children's needs, dreams, purposes, goals, wants, desires, mental health, physical health, self-worth, and functioning were deemed of no importance, and their value was diminished to the evil pleasure experienced by their abusers. As an older woman, my needs, dreams, purpose, goals, wants, desires, mental and physical health, self-worth, and functioning have also been deemed of no importance as I was systematically groomed for exploitation.

As a thirty-two year old, I was admitted to the maternity ward as an "elderly" multipara (a woman who has had more than one pregnancy). Many first-time mothers in Australia are categorized medically as an elderly nulliipara (one who has never given birth), as they have the audacity to delay childbearing until their mid-thirties. A woman with half a century of life expectancy is already hearing that she is "elderly," as her biological clock ticks down to extinction. For the forty-year-old woman with more than half her life yet to live, the grooming is as yet unacknowledged but is pervasive and unrelenting.

Who groomed me, and for what purpose? To answer the "who" is easy: everybody—society, government, media, children, employers, my family of origin, my in-laws, Dan, and business. For what purpose: follow the dollar. An economy that has on standby a workforce of some 5 per cent (ages between sixty-five and eighty) has in-built worker adaptability and flexibility. At a moment's notice, I could be phoned to take on the care of a grandchild unable to attend school or childcare through illness. I could go to school on demand to pick up a child.

Examining the sick-child scenario, obvious benefits abound. As employees, my children were content their child was well cared for; their employer remained ignorant there was any problem; security of employment was not threatened, as their personal caring responsibilities were minimised. The rare request to take leave because "her grandmother wasn't able to because she had to take grandfather to the hospital" was readily accepted. There was no cost to the business and no effect on the bottom-line, shareholders' dividends were not decreased through lowering of profit, and production continued unabated. A promotion position was not compromised. There was no upward pressure on wages as the worker did not need to pay for emergency care so did not need to factor this in when negotiating in the next wages round, individually or as part of a union or group. I provided hundreds of hours of unpaid child minding. This was provided without any demand for wages or benefits, and with no complaint when the job was finished.

I wondered what cultural values had groomed me to accept such a submissive role. Grooming was subtle. The whole process took years of preparation. The "yes set" was wielded against me. I had not demurred but had to acknowledge the scientific fact. I read how tens of thousands of dollars was spent on IVF in an attempt to counter the fact that is normal within the human population for 15 per cent of couples to be infertile. In fact, it never occurred to me to deny it. It affected me as I congratulated myself for having had children earlier so that I effectively diminished myself in my own eyes as I gave heed to my value being linked with my reproduction.

A woman did not expect to live into her sixties, as the average life expectancy was fifty years in 1900. A woman's declining fertility mirrored her diminishing societal value as a child bearer. By 1950, life expectancy had risen to sixty-three and by 2000 to seventy-five, so my nana and mother had died fairly on cue. However, I saw a new scenario as possible for me for the last quarter of my life with a life expectancy nearer ninety, even if society has not altered its vision of me at all. I first had to recognise how I had been influenced to accept a paradigm that was so restrictive before I could attempt to invent myself, even if it was in opposition to all around me.

I was supposed to continue into the twilight, my goals, aspirations, spirituality, and needs subsumed to the greater economic good that would allow sons and daughters to strut the world stage or earn an income at the local shops as I provided unpaid and undervalued backstage assistance. With media support, science reiterating it, as a woman, the completion of my lifespan from menarche to menopause marched me to the conclusion that my continued value to society was restricted to my nurturing my family. Now it appeared the march was to the end of my mortality.

Stories in seniors' magazines that glorified grandmothers who cared for their grandchildren irritated me. Reading superannuation newsletters' articles to assist their readers in claiming any benefits or arranging their finances to budget for the added expense had not created in me an acceptance of this as normal behaviour. I rejected the wisdom or fairness of burdening the baby-boomer generation with the raising of their grandchildren because they have had the temerity to still be alive.

Grooming or conditioning is endemic in relationships, and while the differential of power is now obvious with sexual abuse, it is not fully recognised in this instance. Feminists deconstructed what was seen as normal behaviour but had the effect of psychologically manipulating young women for the benefit of men. It is in early stages of recognition in relation to the older woman. The paradox is that every feminist has a mother. Daughters may not want their mothers to be feminists though they demand the right for themselves.

Each subtle murmuring went largely unchallenged for years by me. I had almost accepted with submission my victimhood. My role in society was being valued for what my uterus produced thirty or forty years earlier. Attacks on those who had not reproduced were vicious. I witnessed with despair as in Australia in 2010 we elected our first female prime minister, Julia Gillard. She was subjected to continual attacks over how she dressed, the style of her haircut, the cut of her jacket, her lifestyle choice of living in a de facto relationship, and of having no children, implying she could not or would not know how families functioned. Her religious beliefs or lack of convention were impugned in ways male prime ministers never suffered. Australia had female suffrage and the right to vote since 1903, but it took longer than a century for us to elect a female to the top job in politics, and then we crucified her. This was Australian misogyny at its best.

I found the attack on baby boomers who have rolled through the psyche of the nation for nearly seventy years tiresome. As a member of the leading edge of the tsunami, I have felt accused of overwhelming first its maternity wards, baby clinics, kindergartens, primary schools, high schools, workplaces, and universities, and then insatiably consuming housing and green spaces around its cities.

Labelled as belonging to the wealthiest generation in Australia's history, economists have berated my generation for pushing up house prices and preventing first-time homebuyers from getting into the property market. My children's generation is touted as having being unfairly disadvantaged by us. I think the problem is that we have had the audacity to not die.

Whereas my friends insisted their children pay their university fees upfront, one of the reasons I continued to work was to pay the mortgage for one of my children undertaking tertiary studies. Initially I assisted my children by investing in houses they could rent at a minimal market rate and then lent some of them money for home deposits or to offset against their mortgages. My girlfriend told me it was a bad idea and was worried it would cause disharmony and jealousy within the family.

It is great they all graduated to good jobs and now are happily married employed parents with homes and careers. Where is the line between encouraging and supporting one's children and over-giving that is reminiscent of a child buying friendship? I don't believe I would have forgone the use of over a hundred thousand dollars of income or the loss of tens of thousands of dollars I could have gained from investing cash if I had not had the underlying belief that I was not good enough and the resultant anxiety that motivated lending so much. I am not the only parent to have done this. A client reported that he remortgaged his house repeatedly to fund his children's lives and he was highly anxious and had low self-esteem. Like him, my assistance was not restricted to education and housing, but covered help with holidays and cars.

Is this financial elder abuse? It certainly was a form of financial bullying, but I was not able to label it, though I felt uncomfortable and attempted on a number of occasions with different recipients to renegotiate my assistance. When two of my children repaid various amounts I had loaned it was a great relief to me. It surprised me that a daughter-in-law had interpreted my providing these loans as indicative of my being very well off. My father had loaned us money when we bought a new car to accommodate our large family. I wonder if this was yet another instance of my doing the same as my parents? My father never lent money to my sister, so I had wanted to be more equitable in my largesse! With so many children this stretched my resources.

Discussion around inheritances saw me aim to provide as much to each future beneficiary as if I had only two children, as I did not want them disadvantaged in comparison to my peers' smaller families. Did I feel guilt about having too many children? We accumulated enough of various household goods so each would have the same quantity. This was so ridiculous. They probably would not even like our choices. I had accepted a false premise that my wealth did not belong to me but was the rightful inheritance of my children.

I even used the term *SKIing*, standing for "spending the kids' inheritance." My daughter enjoyed hearing about any jewellery I purchased. We were concerned that any special pieces should remain in the family. She gave me a copy of her last will and testament. She had detailed in over a page of instructions how she would protect my jewellery and guard it for the next hundred years.

This is reminiscent of the tradition of primogeniture, where the firstborn son inherits the family estate. A friend informed me this still operates especially where there are rural properties involved as he discovered after his brother inherited the farm. This was at such variance with what I had told my mother when she wavered about buying a large television. Her eyesight had deteriorated, and she couldn't see her little screen clearly. She wondered if it was worthwhile, as she thought she didn't have many years left to live. At least for the last five months of her life she was able to view her favourite programs. Discussion around "who would inherit what" occurred before I was even sixty and the kids were in their twenties. It felt like I was a custodian of their money.

The sense of entitlement has so permeated our culture that courts have become involved in this in the last few years, with laws being passed to protect so-called entitled beneficiaries from indignant testators. Although I was distressed when my father threatened to disinherit me, I accepted it was his right.

I shuddered when I realised I had been complicit in perpetuating the demeaning of older women by omission if not commission. I enjoyed a coffee with my ninety-year-old neighbour. She had ordered and paid for the coffee and brought the numbered flag to our table. When we were served, the young waitress only looked at me and only spoke to me, holding her head tilted with the back of her head to my elderly friend. It was so rude. I did not point this out, but to my shame, I tacitly accepted it.

I thought of the many times I have put myself in the "old" basket: I am too old for that. I don't do things like that anymore, because I am too old. I don't have the energy of a young person because I am too old. I can't wear that; it is too young for me. I am old and fat. My eyes aren't as good as they used to be. I can't see that well anymore. I am too old, too old, too old …

I could not resist buying the fridge magnet.

> *How old would you be if you didn't know how old you are?*
>
> —*Satchel Paige*

At the age of forty-two, Leroy Robert "Satchel" Paige was the oldest rookie to play baseball in the Major League in the United States.

Having lost weight and focusing on my health, I rebuffed the influence of the numerous newspaper articles and government policy papers that predicted dire consequences for aged care, hospitals, and the economy from the expected impact of diabetes, obesity, and dementia despite our being touted as the healthiest generation ever. I am not eagerly anticipating becoming a resident in an aged-care facility and work on reducing the risk factors.

Visiting a relative in 2012, I was devastated at her deterioration and loneliness. Driving up the hill to the aged-care home, I had been impressed with its grandeur, it being a lovely Edwardian Tudor-style mansion in Maine overlooking the sea. A previous visit several years earlier had been a joy. She chirped away like her little pet parrot, Charlie, but a stroke had reduced her to dependence on strangers, with no living relatives in America.

Sitting among twenty other residents in a large circle in various types of chairs and lounges, I did not recognise her. She was crumpled over, with eyes closed. "Not having a good day," apologised the nurse. I went through the photo-book her grandniece had sent over, depicting all her Australian relatives over the years. She was so sad. I touched her cheek gently, willing some warmth into her, but terrified that a kind touch might remind her of what she no longer had, though I was unwilling to deprive her and myself of the connection.

Carers were going around the room offering drinks of tea and juice. One lady was enjoying having her nails being painted. I noticed Aunt's fingernails were varnished a pale pink and carefully manicured. Her hair was combed neatly, and she was comfortably dressed. The television was quite loud so the residents could hear it, but it interfered with conversation, effectively preventing it. Perhaps other activities were undertaken at different times and in different settings, but there was no evidence to suggest that happened. It broke my heart leaving her there.

Twelve years earlier I had left my mother in a nursing home. Although she was there for a relatively short period for rehabilitation after a heart attack, the desperate eagerness she showed to be visited showed me how lonely such places can be. I don't believe I will ever feel the need to hurry into a similar environment, aware it may trigger distress in me from the memories I have of feeling abandoned and powerless in hospital when I was six and seven.

There is such a sense of powerlessness involved when a fastidious woman like Aunt was expected to use disposable pants because it was too labour intensive to take all the residents to a toilet. I inwardly cringed that such institutionalised elder abuse is tolerated. Society in general and families in particular are not always willing to pay the real cost of care for the vulnerable people that created the society and raised the children. The concern is often expressed about not being forced to sell the family home to pay for care, as if it belongs to children who haven't lived in it for decades.

As my children rushed with greater speed into childrearing, I felt the pressure for the relegation of my aspirations to the shelf: peer pressure to retire, to enjoy my grandchildren, to travel. After all, if there is no financial need to work, the question was, why would you? The grandchildren are only little for such a short time, I was told, and if you want to travel overseas, I was advised to do it while you are well, and don't forget the tremendous increase in the price of travel insurance once you are older than seventy!

I was aware of the disquiet I had felt for many years bubbling up into my conscious awareness, no longer quietened by my overeating. Like other women of my generation, I was formed in one era and created another. I married a man raised in that earlier era too.

I observed my sons sharing the care of their newborns, and being emotionally close with their children, spending time with them from birth and during their earliest years in a way their father had not. I noted the difference. I wondered why it took both parents to change a nappy. They cooked and shared tasks all the time. They enjoyed their friends together and separately with no problem. They organised separate holidays but spent a lot of time camping together. Holidays were a priority, and they all regularly drove off to the local coastal holiday spots, inviting their siblings and friends to join them.

I was grateful Daniel hung out nappies when no one else in the neighbourhood did, but like all the men I knew, he never changed one for our babies. One night when I was quite ill, and our firstborn was three months old, he still refused to change the nappy. He claimed he did not know how. Thankfully, he did assist when they were older, as a couple of the boys had bedwetting problems until the end of primary school.

> At a funeral of a colleague, an acquaintance of forty years' standing spoke with me about her ultimatum twelve months earlier to her husband. Having been a business owner employing fifty people, she had baulked at the expectation of fitting into a role where she was again the housewife in retirement. She was not going to revert to a role where she was dependant on her husband emotionally, financially, or in any other way. Either he accepted that or "she was out of there." He did. She stayed and is having a ball. She stated you have to be wary of the quiet, emotionally controlling men.

I recalled this when I saw that son, now an adult, changing my grandson's nappy and playing with him, knowing he does most of the cooking. He has altered greatly from the wisecracking twelve-year-old who refused to do a chore because it was "woman's work." One evening, his little son, age two, demanded his father change his nappy. This it seems was very much my grandson's preference at that moment. At three, he had great hand and eye coordination, and his vocabulary and insight were remarkable. My son says he spends a great deal of time with his little boy playing with him, in contrast to what he says he experienced.

Visiting another son days after the birth of his first child, I followed him to the nursery, where he competently changed a dirty diaper. It was so expected to be part of his fathering it deserved no comment, so I didn't. I was impressed.

Daniel saw himself as the provider. He had been raised in a two-bedroom cottage that was the standard after the Second World War ended. As a baby boomer with a four-bedroom home, an en-suite bathroom, and a family room, he had a higher standard of living than where the bathroom was an annex and the toilet was outside. The "dunny man" was a fixture of the childhoods of many Australian baby boomers, as he carried the receptacle on his shoulder down the driveway to remove the contents into a sewerage truck.

He expressed the traditional role of breadwinner through bargain hunting and shopping. He loved to share information about where the best bargains on meat specials were, texting his sons like the hunter might signal the village of the whereabouts of game or the fisherman where the fish are biting in the local bay.

Raised to be a traditional provider but like many others, Dan married a woman who had a much wider role in society than his or my mother ever did. Our mothers worked outside the home too, as the labour-saving devices of vacuum cleaners, washing machines, and easy-care clothes all contributed to freeing them from the hours formerly required for household chores. However, greater educational opportunities allowed me to develop a career and contribute substantially to accumulating assets. I was no longer as financially dependent upon his accumulation of goods and chattels and I did not want to be included amongst them.

I recognised there has been a huge change from before the Second World War to now in how men and the wider Australian society viewed the role of husband and father, but it was insufficient to explain why, within the primary relationship of my life, I had felt I was not good enough. I had stopped emotional eating. I was experiencing the emotions that had been hidden from my awareness in their very raw state. I did not like what I had seen or felt.

I searched books and internet sites and talked to friends to label what I saw. Without the labels, it was as if I could not see what had happened to me. Old, culturally accepted forms of being the head of the family were revealed as emotionally abusive in light of modern understanding of the effect on a woman's self-esteem, confidence, and independence. As Pat Craven, who worked with abusive men in the UK as a parole officer, wrote in *Living with the Dominator*, that although everyone believes an abused woman knows she is being abused, the reality is she is in the midst of "a very confusing mess and that it must be somehow her fault" (Craven, 5). This certainly was true for me. Non-physical abuse is even more confusing than when bruises are left.

I was concerned that as I had married in the Catholic Church, I was in a different category from other women. However, unexpectedly for me, I found that the change in awareness at a cultural level reflected the advances in understanding of what constituted a valid marriage. For a valid marriage to be formed always depended upon equality of partners and sharing of resources. In the Canon Law of the Catholic Church, this is stated in terms of the ground for annulment, where there is a grave lack of discretion of judgement (Canon 1095, 2). This canon deals with the essential rights and obligations within marriage. Questions include whether a person understands that respect and not abuse is part of marriage and whether both parties participate in a partnership of life. Having a wedding performed in a Catholic Church celebrated by a priest did not obliterate the obligation to respect one's spouse or to be respected.

The last stage of principled conscience defined by Kohlberg, whose work I first mentioned in the chapter on my childhood, is one he stated was rarely developed. He did not believe many people developed principles that they would actually suffer for rather than betray. Having often found myself at odds with the prevailing culture around me, perhaps I inadvertently propelled myself into considering the moral dilemmas that promoted growth.

Working It Through

Identify any times in your life when you felt powerless, helpless, not in control, unimportant, detached, demeaned, or manipulated.

Who was the other person involved? Did this reinforce in you a long-held negative belief about yourself? What is that negative belief?

Roles in Marriage

Working in schools and later in a private practice, boys and men explained the importance of games in their lives. The people males counted as friends were the people with whom they played. The games changed, though not always the players. At seven it was handball; at eleven, football; as a teen, it was how popular they were with girls; in the twenties, with whom they drank beer. As professionals, tradesmen, businessmen, retailers, or athletes, the game was being better, stronger, faster, or more *something* than the other guy.

Translated into marriage, this attitude implies a power imbalance where the male dominates the female. However, if marriage is seen as a game, there has been a vast change in the awareness of what those rules are that provide the guidelines for couples. It is now recognised that roles are less rigidly defined, and there is awareness in Australian society of a greater emphasis on an equal partnership and in creating and sharing resources and promoting a mutual emotional nurturing.

Chores seem to be a way of expressing this egalitarianism. For some, there seems little acknowledgement that the knowledge of the game has changed and therefore should the rules. Old rules do not work. Unfortunately, while the awareness of one partner may have evolved, the other may remain mired in expectations from many decades earlier, formed within their family of origin by their experiences of school, church, and society.

When you view romantic movies with your partner, how do you feel? Is it unbearably quiet? Can you look at each other? Can you talk about the problems in the relationships depicted on the screen, or are they too close?

When it comes to arguments, problems in communication between you, moods, emotions, or issues of discomfort, who brings it up? Who notices there is a problem? Who shares how he or she is feeling? Who always takes the lead?

Are the roles in marriage rigid or flexible?

Have there been many changes in the roles in your marriage?

When did the changes occur?

What changes would you like to happen? Have you tried to negotiate these changes? What happened?

Did your partner perceive marriage differently from courtship? Is courtship a different game demanding different rules? When the game changes to marriage, do the rules change too? How has or will retirement affect your roles?

Sometimes it can be immediate. Following a Catholic wedding ceremony, in which a man promised his bride, before the priest and her family, to raise his children as Catholics, once inside the car as they were leaving, he told her that would be the last time she would ever see the inside of a church.

Another sat his wife down after the honeymoon and told her a long list of dos and don'ts, as she was now a married woman: no makeup, no single friends, and no going out. Even though she gave definite and defiant nos to these statements, being Catholic, and believing that being married was for life, it took her many years to reach the point of leaving.

One young woman noticed it occurred over a period of time as her first wedding anniversary loomed. She said it was like he took the list of pros and cons for being married and gradually crossed off all the pros.

Are there expectations on how you should behave as you have matured? Who has these expectations? Are they your expectations or another's?

Do you remember when you weren't old enough? What does that feel like now? Feel the excitement in your chest, the anticipation? Note the look in your eye, the smile as you wait. What was it for? Was it for your first bicycle, your first high heels, going out on your first date, getting your driver's licence, receiving your first football or cricket bat, being old enough to join the local team, or becoming an altar boy, having your first beer?

Consider in how many ways society, through the media and through government policies, tells you how old you are, or by focusing on what disabilities you have results in you and everyone else believing you are unworthy of being looked after.

How often do your peers and children reinforce this? If you doubt this, I challenge you to note it over the next few weeks. I have no doubt it will become obvious to you and you will wonder how you failed to notice.

Consequences for breaking rules can range from a passive-aggressive response, where there is no answer to a question or action on a request, a withdrawal, or can be as overt as one woman's experience of being sat down with her family and his, with everyone joining in, telling her what she was doing wrong. Of course, sadly, physical intimidation and violence are all too common as we see in the headlines every day.

Every person acts for a reason.

Looking for the reason your partner does something requires looking at the end result. If you want to make a baby happy, you might tickle her. If you know tickling her makes her cry, and you still tickle her, you intend the baby to cry.

If you have reacted a thousands times to your partner's actions in the same way, your partner knows this and intends you to react that way. It may take a long time to accept that someone you love knows how you will react and intentionally elicits that negative reaction.

We can spend a lifetime believing that a group of people, such as men think differently and don't understand, but that is to protect us from recognising the implications of their deliberate intent. If he knows a small gift thrills you, his withholding is deliberate. Men understand cause and effect on the playing field very well. They understand cause and effect in their actions in relationships.

Take any episode that bothers you, past or present. Write down what was happening beforehand, what action he took, you took, and what was the result. Discuss this with someone not emotionally involved who can look at the event dispassionately.

Like another young woman, warned the day she came home from her honeymoon that as she was a married woman now, she could not have male friends and could not go out with girlfriends, have you been told that it is inappropriate with whom you socialise? Have there been restrictions placed on your social life? How old would you feel if this happened? Has anything like that happened to you? Did you mean to give anyone else control over whom you were "allowed" to have as friends?

Float back in your imagination through your years, down your timeline. Are there unspoken rules to your relationship? Have you agreed to them explicitly, or acted as if you agree simply because you could no longer fight?

By contrast, are there things other people do that you would like to, but you don't because of disapproval?

From my journal, December 25, 2012

Dust lies deep, dormant over the heart of the land.
The earth breathes, stirring to life.
Swirling, it rifts and roils, recreating familiar patterns,
Seeping under the doors, blinding the children, deadening all.
Seared, scorching the tumbleweeds,
the fallen wood floating across the land,
the devouring flame.
Seasons die and then spattering rain
Sweeps aside the rivulet and then flood,
All debris, scoring channels anew,
Forcing through the mud, new life,
Lush with growth nurturing the healthy whole.

Chapter 8

REPAIR OR RUPTURE, REALISATION, AND RECOVERY

Repair

Sitting in a café after viewing a movie in town, I listened to Dan complain about the size of the portion of fish he was served. It wasn't as much as he usually had. I laughed at that. We had only been going out every Wednesday for a few months, and the epithet of "usual" sounded incongruous to me. Attempting to rebuild communication in the beginning of 2013, we organised outings for each Wednesday, taking turns to pay for the excursion. We visited the zoo, the botanical gardens, the art gallery, and many various tourist spots locally and in nearby country areas. Always finding somewhere pleasant to lunch, we had plenty of time to reconnect.

I knew in my twenties I was good at ignoring my feelings. However, ignored feelings still affected me. They provided motivation for my behaviour. For a long time I had forgotten I had emotions I ignored, and I certainly wasn't aware of what those emotions were.

Now I knew what those emotions were. I was anxious and lonely. I needed to deal with them directly. I thought that if I did not feel so lonely, I would not be as anxious.

The next day, I walked up to him in as he climbed off a ladder, having replaced a light bulb. I told him I appreciated when I needed something done, and his response was to do it fairly immediately, ranging from replacing a light globe, fixing up something that had gone wrong with my computer, or binding some papers into a book. I made the suggestion that each day we could tell each other something we liked about the other. He didn't feel he needed to do that as he had no problem with self-esteem.

Out in the garden, I began to choose to garden near Dan. If he was sitting down on the veranda, I went out to sit next to him. I compromised on the selection of television programs. I sat through movies I didn't really want to watch, though I refused the Japanese/Chinese martial art type ones outright. For the first time in my life, I took him to a cricket match. I organised flights and accommodation so he could watch the Australian team play at the MCG (Melbourne Cricket Ground).

I wanted to talk about dreams and goals and what we had achieved and how we saw the next twenty years panning out. I wanted a greater connectedness. I wanted to know that when one of us was dying, the other would be there, that we would be looking into each other's eyes with a deep satisfaction and sense of our souls' journeys together.

April 28, 2013: the priest spoke about premature twins, Brielle and Kyrie Jackson of Westminster, Massachusetts, USA, born in 1995. The smaller at two pounds was failing; her legs and arms stick thin, her skin bluish grey, gasping for breath, and nothing the doctors did was helping, whereas her sister born at two pound three ounces was thriving. When they were a month old, against hospital policy, a nurse placed the healthier baby into the other's incubator—"double bedding" was how she described it. From that moment, the healthier sister snuggled into her sister and calmed her, and the sick twin began to flourish.

"We all have a need for physical touch," he said. "Four hugs for survival, eight for maintenance, and twelve for growth." He suggested we give the person next to us a hug. Of course I did. It was a one-sided hug, with me putting my arms around my partner of nearly fifty years and him not moving, standing with his arms straight down beside his body.

After the service, a woman approached me in the car park, first asking if I was well. She said she didn't want to say how wonderful I looked only to find out I was dying. She had seen me the previous week, and like many others, had noticed a big difference in me.

A friend I knew well approached at the same time, joining in with the congratulations on my weight loss. Meanwhile, as was his want, Dan left to wait in the car. They really wanted to know what I had done, and I briefly told them and mentioned the benefits to my health and the fact that I had solved my emotional eating, to which one of them exclaimed she did that!

I shared that I was writing a book about it, having been inspired by the lay preacher from the previous year when he looked directly at me and said, "Write that book!" in response to the question he had posed of, "What would you do if Jesus came to you today?" I told them I also knew what the book would be about, where moments before it had never occurred to me. They gave each other a hug and we all hugged. They both lived alone, and we talked about hugs from grandchildren being the only sort of hugs they now received.

A week later Dan was hospitalised for a minor procedure. When he was brought home, I went through into the kitchen to say hello to everyone and took my grandchild into my arms. Dan stood there and made no move toward me. Despite numerous opportunities, he made no movement toward me then, nor a touch, a kiss, or a hug in the following weeks. I didn't do it deliberately, but it shouted out how much physical contact between us was left up to me. I felt it in my gut; it was very uncomfortable. My throat was very tight too. I recognized that because of those body sensations, I usually had eaten or "made amends" by approaching him though touching, kissing, acknowledging him, and inviting him to be sexually intimate with me.

I found I could no longer touch his shoulder or his hand or indeed any part of him as I passed. Putting scraps into a bin became a weird, disjointed dance with his moving away from me if I came toward him in the kitchen if he was in front of the sink where the bin was.

I was not quite sure what this meant, but I was struggling with the future, something I hadn't experienced since I was twenty-two.

Five Love Languages

I did not read Dr. Gary Chapman's book *The Five Love Languages* until after I had separated from Dan. I spent the previous six months investing emotionally, physically, financially, and spiritually in the relationship. I am satisfied I did this, knowing I did everything I could to prevent the dissolution of what had been grown over my entire adult life. I walked away knowing there was absolutely nothing left undone that may have worked. Dr. Chapman provides a framework for the methods I employed when I attempted to repair my relationship with my spouse.

Dr. Chapman describes five types of love languages. A love language, put simply, is how we express our love for others and how we receive it. We all have different ways we let people know that we love them. We all have different ways we experience being loved. It's important to know how you and your partner express and receive love so you don't experience misunderstandings in an intimate relationship. It is also very useful in other personal relationships.

The first mode he mentions is that of demonstrating love through physical touch. I was reminded that Daniel wrote before we were married about the necessity of physical touch to preserve a relationship. When our relationship began, I didn't notice the difference in the level of intimacy through the use of touch. Touch was often confused with sex and guilt. It seemed we couldn't "get enough of each other," but this wasn't the case. I did not recognise his discomfort in the amount of touch I needed. The need for touch mirrors the bond between a mother and neonate.

I knew one of my children did not enjoy being cuddled the way the other children did. When only four months old, I resorted to standing, rocking the baby in my arms while he suckled at the breast. He weaned at ten months, where his siblings loved being cuddled and breastfed, most not weaning until into their third year of life. I enjoyed the physical interdependency with my babies and was not interested in early weaning.

Observing my adult offspring, I note that the same propensity for expressing love physically through touch remains as true now as it was in their babyhoods. The son that loved being carried in a baby sling still expresses his love of his grown sons and his infant children through snuggling and hugs. The toddler who wriggled with delight as I massaged his chubby arms and legs still seeks touch and has a loving physical presence with his wife and infant. He also gives the most wonderful hugs to his mother. The one who was tactile defensive still resists touch even with his offspring.

Acts of service, Chapman's second mode, are understood as expressions of love. They can be quite simple. When Dan gave me a cup of tea, I told him I understood that was to show he loved me. I then asked him to give me a kiss on the neck or a pat on the bum! Using Chapman's terms, I can now acknowledge that touch was not his choice of expressing love but may have caused him discomfort, hence his rush to introduce our grandsons to the manly art of handshaking before their first birthdays. To cater to each other, I encouraged him to expand his repertoire. I loved making that special lemon meringue pie. I appreciated the cutting of a hedge or ringing to ask if I needed bread or milk.

Quality time should not be reserved exclusively for children. Couples need it too. Spending uninterrupted time together is important, but possibly it was more essential for Daniel than me. Hours spent next to each other doing Sudoku or in front of the television lost their appeal, and I could not do it anymore.

A fourth mode of sharing love is through the giving of gifts. Gifts as celebration is one aspect, but the little unexpected gifts of a scarf, a pot of tulips, a pair of gloves, or some notepaper can far outweigh the expensive ring given as a Christmas present to be shown off in answer to the inevitable, "And what did you get for Christmas?"

In 1969, when away teaching in a small country town, I sent little gifts to Dan, but I stopped when he told me this was wasting money. I embroidered a handkerchief for him and reassured him he didn't have to use it, but I liked showing him in a different way that I loved him.

Buying gifts was an important means for me to express love. I bought a little dress and frilly leggings for a granddaughter the other day, and a baby-cloth rattle for an expectant mum. I disagreed with him that I was spoiling them, and that I was spending too much. Before our firstborn was months old, I emphatically argued with him that the children did not have to wait until they went to school to find out about gifts at birthdays and Christmas, but I always struggled to justify presents for them.

"Words of affirmation" sounds like an amazingly complex description for saying something pleasant to your partner about him or her.

It is important to determine what language is predominating a person's repertoire if you wish to communicate that you love someone. When I fell in love with Dan, I experienced a physical closeness that resonated with the infant within me, reminding me of the warmth of that initial bonding I had experienced with my mother. Just as the young child learns to speak, all I initially required was conversation to recreate what I knew from my early childhood relationship with her. Rather than creating emotional intimacy with Dan, a codependent relationship developed. It was a chicken and an egg situation. I was anxious and I had a huge need for approval that I felt I did not receive. That need for approval constantly evoked anxiety within me.

In her book, *Codependency for Dummies*, Darlene Lancer exquisitely teased out the difference between emotional intimacy and codependency. In order to develop true emotional intimacy, Dan and I needed to take the risk to express our true feelings without considering the consequences, to be able to show our feelings of vulnerability as they occurred, and to acknowledge our differences without projecting and reacting to them.

Although codependency is often referred to with regards to drugs and alcohol, it should be applied to a far wider context. Darlene Lancer noted codependent behaviour would exist prior to an alcoholic marriage and would continue even after alcohol is given away. This is relevant for any substance abuse or addiction. Not unusually in Australia,[17] for many people, alcoholism may be a problem. The addiction can be behavioural. It can be gambling, hoarding, Internet porn, sex, shopping or a myriad other things. The essential nature is the anxiety caused when one partner is dependent on the other for approval not the behaviour.

Rupture

I was worried. I was no longer emotionally eating and had to deal with the anxiety and its causes.

---

[17] In Australia, ranked around twenty-fifth in the world for alcohol consumption, the expectation when visiting friends for dinner, having a party, or throwing a barbeque is that there will be copious amounts of alcohol brought by guests and provided by hosts. In the United States, a friend tells me that a man might bring a six-pack of beers or a bottle of wine. In Australia he is more likely to arrive with a "slab" of twenty-four cans of beer, a bottle of spirits, and two bottles of wine. The guest will also have access to his host's fridge and cellar should he "run out." With the greater awareness in the twenty-first century of the impact of alcohol on one's capacity to drive a car, younger generations have grown up understanding the need to have a designated driver. Alternatively, there is greater acceptance of taking a taxi home and fetching the car next day.

Dan complained about the remake of an old movie we went to see, saying he couldn't understand it and asking why they didn't put the same heads on the actors as in the original so he could follow it better. I didn't feel like laughing. I was worried about his memory and wondered if there was something more sinister happening. On June 3, 2013 I discussed this and other behaviours with my doctor, who referred me to his doctor. I was very anxious about Dan's health and she referred me to a psychologist to help me deal with my "anxiety as a result of her husband's behaviour. He possibly has dementia but has been unwilling to get any help."

For instance he seemed to have no ability to refrain from spending thousands of dollars on cricket memorabilia. I asked Dan how much money he had spent. He gave a figure that was a third of what I knew it had to be and was in fact a fifth. The next day I sat down next to him. I had waited twenty-four hours for him to be truthful. His response was that I should not have been snooping. I had accessed his memorabilia database. He had recorded all his purchases, with dates of purchase, cost price, descriptions, what room they were in the house, or if he had lent them out and from where he had bought them. He even had photographs of each item. I explained I was worried that he was mishandling our finances and that I had a right as his wife to know, as it would affect our retirement.

I was not going to be financially bullied anymore. I told Dan I could not stay another twenty years in the relationship if things continued the way they were. I would not tolerate his buying any more cricket memorabilia. The house was severely overcrowded. I found the collection hideous. Every wall, including those in bathrooms and the laundry were crowded with pieces from his collection. Framed cricket bats abounded. Caps and baggy greens were prized. Faces of cricketers replaced family photographs I had once displayed. Shelves were crowded with DVDs he had made from recorded cricket games and interviews. Cricketing books and cricket magazines were piled on every surface.

Nor could I tolerate the way he was spending money in retaliation to what I was buying or doing. I was shocked to find that during the years I had taken in boarders he had spent over fifteen thousand dollars. His annual income at the time was not much more and we had five children attending private schools. This was in the years when housing interest rates in Australia hit 17 per cent and he had told me taking in boarders would help. I made a copy of his database and was appalled at the amount he had spent. He had always told me each item had been inexpensive. It never occurred to me to query him. He promised half a dozen times to cease adding to his collection, acknowledging we had no room to display any more. However items would be delivered and if I was not at home, they were sometimes stored in the garage until he chose to bring them into the house months later.

Dan's desire was to set up a gallery for the Daniel Heartley Cricket Collection or to donate it to a museum in his name. Institutions may have accepted some items, but as there was no consistent theme and many items were not worth half their cost, I was advised that unless there was a substantial sum to fund the costs of curating the collection and provision of a suitable venue, no institution would accept the donation.

He was quite knowledgeable. He loved visiting memorabilia shops, cricketing grounds and museums. I reluctantly spent hours standing beside him as he and other enthusiasts exchanged details and statistics. I was astounded that he researched any district we were visiting in Australia or overseas. A special shop or museum appeared "unexpectedly" or was "just around the corner". In London I had organised to do some historical research. I understood he was going to help me. However he disappeared for hours, returning with an item that cost a thousand pounds. I decided we couldn't afford for me to do any research!

I spent hours talking with him, baring my soul, and I could no longer overlook his dismissal of this with statements that he couldn't remember anything I said and didn't want to remember. I would not tolerate his refusal to talk with me or to ever touch me, even non-sexually. I no longer would look for excuses.

The bond withered and died. I had yet to decide, but I now knew it was my choice to stay or go. My decisions were no longer being driven by emotions that were pushed out of my awareness. I had paid for the promised holiday overseas, so I resolved to stay at least until then with the hope that possibly Dan would want to work on our relationship with me. I also needed to learn if there was a possibility of dementia. If there was, I imagined it would drastically alter the situation. Dan made an appointment for his brain scan but cancelled it.

Decades ago, discussing marriage with my girlfriend and her husband, the issue of what constituted crossing the line was aired. For my girlfriend, it was either of them having an affair. For some the line is gambling. A relative preferred to budget with the surety of welfare payments than to be unable to feed her children because their father had gambled away that week's wages. Being locked out of the home on a winter's night was the final straw for one, when being locked in, without food or phone, deprived of her liberty terrified another and resulted in her leaving after twenty-eight years of an emotionally abusive marriage. Threats of self-harm imprisoned one woman in a relationship. Another saw the line when she could not protect her toddler from witnessing her husband slitting open his abdomen.

I can't remember if I contributed an opinion. I did not know I had a line that if he crossed meant for me that I would leave. As a mother of a large family, my fear had always been he might leave me, as he had three times before marriage. It was not that he in any manner threatened to leave. It was my fear. On holiday I found the line.

I had seen advertisements on the television that the reason there needs to be women's refuges is that the period when a woman leaves an abusive relationship is most dangerous as the abuser seeks to exert control then, in an attempt to regain dominance. I had not applied that to my situation. Daniel was not physically abusive. I had not been locked in a dungeon.

Nevertheless, Dan reacted in a physical way that can easily be interpreted as his asserting his dominance even though he disputes that. I spent forty-seven years with someone who has disputed my reality. My thoughts, feelings, viewpoints have suffered dismissal so frequently that in order to maintain certainty I have often written about my experiences. Notes on my smart phone and emails to friends sometimes suffice.

I told him on the morning of July 4 that he "broke" me. In the words from an email I sent a girlfriend at that time, three "nights of keeping me awake for three hours when I had not recovered in any way from lack of sleep from our flights over, supposedly giving me what I had asked for, he making an effort, while (a relative) is in the bed next to me, completely humiliated and distressed me. Trying to talk to him about how inappropriate this was and is has resulted in his present lack of comprehension. … it nearly did my mind in totally. I felt totally abused, keeping quiet" to stop waking anyone else. "I feel I will be prostituting myself to stay."

My girlfriend responded most distressed. She advised me to get the other person and come home. Still unsure if I was dealing with a man in early stages of dementia, I acted the way I always did, which was to act as if nothing had happened in front of other people. When we had shared accommodation with others on previous trips there had never been any such problem, let alone three times when he was given a very clear "no" the following mornings when we were alone.

During the mediation process for the divorce and property settlement, when asked what had caused the end of the marriage, Dan characterised these events as attempting to be intimate in response to what I had asked. I love the animated cartoon by blogger Rockstar Dinosaur Pirate Princess depicting "Consent. It's As Simple As Tea". You don't make people drink tea no matter how much trouble you have gone to make it, how much you want to drink tea, or how special you think it is. Why is it so hard to understand?

I had finished being told it was sunny when I could feel the rain. It was time to go.

That Independence Day, I fell in love with and purchased Scott Rogers's beautiful bronze sculpture "The Other Side of Seventeen." She sits with her hand holding her hat at her feet, her legs bent, her chin resting on her knees, eyes glazed with dreams. Accompanying her was a statement he wrote that included the question "What longings are harboured in the hearts of young women?" He saw it as miraculous when a person awakened to "see themselves differently and demand the whole world does as well." She was a promise to me, a talisman.

Less than a month after purchasing my bronze sculpture, while talking with my girlfriend over lunch, I was able to recognise how hopeless it was trying to continue as I was and resolved to end my marriage. When I returned home that afternoon, in answer to Dan's question, I said yes, I was leaving him.

At the beginning of my transpersonal journey, I had not recognised the meaning of Dan's wanting to use the toilet when I cleaned my teeth. I felt ashamed I was irritated. At the end, I recognised that no matter how it looked, even if he could characterise it to himself and others as loving me, it was his not hearing what I was saying, not seeing how I was feeling that showed that there was no empathy for me as a person in my own right.

If I stayed, I would not be true to myself. I would not be showing any respect for myself.

When matters end in violence and headline the news with homicide, many ask why didn't he or she just leave? Perhaps my story might provide some understanding. There are many steps on the continuum that may end in violence. At one end of a relationship there is a mutual respect for each other as individuals, with needs and aspirations. At the other end there is no respect by each for the other.

Where the line is along that continuum for one person is based on their individual histories and values. For the young woman who left when her partner demurred about marrying her, the line was fair and square at the point of mutual respect. For others the incremental change in a relationship along the continuum happens so gradually that it is explained away or ignored until they die. A friend recalled her mother declining into dementia, while saying how many times she had been on the point of leaving her husband. He took her from her deathbed but staff prevented him at the gate of the hospice from taking her home, as he denied her right to leave him.

Emotional eating had pushed knowledge of my emotions out of my conscious awareness. I was only able to ignore how I felt because I overate. I was married. I had kids. I had a house. I had an education. I had a career. As my mother said I hadn't done too badly in life. I had met the goals set when I was twenty. I didn't have me. I had one life and gave it to Daniel. I took it back.

Realisation

> *For some reason, we see divorce as a failure, despite the fact that each of us has a right, and an obligation, to rectify any other mistake we make in life.*
>
> -Dr Joyce Brothers in Amy Poon's *This Little Piggy Got Divorced*

Failing marriage is not a capital offence.

I no longer have to believe there is something inherently wrong with me, wondering if I were younger, thinner, or better in some manner, Dan would want me. After all, when I had all those attributes, the anxiety within the relationship was the same. When I told him yes, I was leaving, he said he had thought about it and decided I could live upstairs and he would live downstairs as it wouldn't make any difference to him. After three weeks, I realised it made a big difference to me and moved out of the house.

I did not plan to separate and divorce, but making the decision to do so felt like the first real decision I had ever made. It wasn't motivated by anxiety that had been pushed out of my awareness. It wasn't motivated by a desire to please or driven by fear to conform to others' expectations, lest they not like me. It wasn't motivated by feelings that I was not good enough and I had to prove I was. It was motivated by realising I respected myself but I wouldn't if I stayed.

In the book *The Top Five Regrets of the Dying* by Australian palliative care nurse Bronnie Ware, the failure to live a life "true to myself" rather than "the life others expected me to live" was the first regret she found the dying expressed. Wishing they had not worked so hard, had the courage to express their feelings, stayed in touch with their friends and let themselves be happier followed. I had no intention of wasting the last quarter of my life fulfilling roles instead of being a person.

One of my sons commented on my new life as a single woman, saying I was "a woman aspiring to be a person." I could only agree. He had not meant it as a compliment.

I have been told I am brave for having decided at "my time of life" that I deserve better. I always deserved better. Such ageism exists because the expectation is that I ought to be weak, sick, poor, and dependent, where the reality is that without the needs of young children, I have so much more energy and health. I can exercise, sleep, and occupy myself in healthy ways unavailable to me when there were demands upon my time and energy by so many others. I have worked through my past choices and seen how they evolved from previous ones that predisposed me to make those choices. I can let go of the pain of choices that no longer work for me as I accept myself and others who have been part of my life journey.

I was not ready for the upheaval but evidently with divorce being on the rise[18] in those over sixty in contrast to the falling divorce rate in all other age groups, it is rather more common than I supposed. I

---

[18] The number of divorces per thousand women over fifty years has increased from 7.6 to 8.9 in the last two decades. Over sixty years, the increase is from 2.1 to 3.6. The drop in the divorce rate for those younger than forty years is affected by the fact that people are older when they marry. (E.g., marriage per thousand women age twenty to twenty-four years has decreased from 60 to 27.1 over the last twenty years.) http://www.abs.gov.au/ausstats/abs@.nsf/Products/3310.0~2012~Chapter~Divorces?OpenDocument.

was very surprised to find the term "the silver separators" had been coined to describe it. This is belittling of mature people and evidence of ageism. I did not even know there was a trend, as if it were some fad. People attempting to determine underlying causes ascribe it to women now being more financially independent, without realising that if the only reason women stay in a marriage is economics, there must be a vast well of soul-bruised females in our community.

Recovery

Forgiving the unrepentant is like drawing pictures in water.
—Japanese proverb

Forgiving without forgetting is like loving without liking.
—Anonymous

Forgiveness has always seemed like something I had to suffer, like a sacrifice. It is a vital social skill, necessary to oil the machinery of social intercourse. This makes sense at the level of being cut off by another car, or given rude service at the shop, garage, or government agency. I would not want to live in a world where people took revenge for every hurt.

It is less about forgiveness than about tolerance. Maybe he didn't see me? Perhaps she had an argument with the boss moments before? With understanding, my belief was I could tolerate the acts that occurred that injured me, or my pride, and my sense of safety. I challenged the little thoughts that arose that inflamed my anger. I dampened the flames with sensible helpful thoughts. A wealth of psychological work is devoted to this to which belong rational emotive therapy and cognitive behavioural therapy.

I decided being tolerant was a ridiculous posture for dealing with life's great hurts. It had allowed me to be walked over. I didn't want to forgive as if I accepted being badly treated rather than defending myself from the evil of being harmed. It wasn't about creating a willingness to accept feelings, habits, or beliefs that were different from my own. I did not want to endure pain or hardship.

When I found myself in an act of unforgiving, the meaning became much clearer. I didn't want to forgive. I wanted to let go of the pain. I had heard that forgiving someone isn't about the other person but it is necessary for healing of oneself. Again, it is about letting go of the emotional pain connected to the memory.

I was indoctrinated with this precept: "But I say to you, do not resist one who is evil. But if anyone strikes you on the right cheek, turn to him the other also; and if anyone would sue you and take your coat, let him have your cloak as well; and if anyone forces you to go one mile, go with him two miles" Matthew 5:39–41).

I didn't want to be struck on any more cheeks. I didn't want to forgive the people who had struck my cheeks. I simply wanted my cheeks to stop hurting.

Oscar Wilde's advice to "Always forgive your enemies; nothing annoys them so much," seemed more fun, but I doubted it was forgiveness as it seems to me that to forgive I needed to let go of many feelings—resentment, hurt, pain, anger, desire for revenge, and disgust are a few that came to mind. If I was in a state where I didn't want to forgive, hoping the recipient would somehow be annoyed, it seemed insufficient motivation for the act of forgiveness, whatever that was.

I wrote fifteen hundred points about which I had negative feelings. I selected one thought, like forgiving myself for not having known myself very well when I married, remembering I thought I did. I can tell myself that I was only twenty-two years old and that is young. People today recognize that a lot of work is done on developing one's identity in the twenties. We now know the brain has not even finished its development. It was going to take a long time to work through the list.

Did I need to forgive the teacher who humiliated me when I was six, my parents for not ever thinking maybe they could have taken me back to my first-grade class to say good-bye before moving to a new school, or for not visiting me in hospital when I was in isolation with scarlet fever at age six? Should I forgive my mother for not paying for anaesthetic whenever I went to the dentist and had painful fillings because one shilling was too expensive?

I had many people to forgive: people for not ever listening to me; for dropping me; for telling me I was boring; for saying when I lost weight that I had "got rid of my ugly bits"; for not noticing how much I gave up; myself for being whom others wanted and not myself; my flatmate for dismissing any further contact with an out-of-sight, out-of-mind, can't-be-bothered attitude; for the other friends I have lost; the school inspector who told me my voice was boring; the teacher who told me to work with my brain and not my hands; the doctor who was more interested in getting home before midnight than assisting me to have a natural birth; the nurse who cut my fingernails when I was six and made me feel I had no right to be pretty; or my mother for calling me a Belsen horror because I was so thin.

The thoughts piled up, washing against my mind like detritus on the shore. I didn't take a red pen to them, to delete what was unacceptable, or petty, or mean. I set aside any judgement of myself for carrying these hurts, some for decades. They had lain there underneath, holding the recent events higher, making them prominent and painful.

I had larger hurts. Some hurts involved others being hurt too. My list grew: professional hurts, personal hurts, childhood hurts, adult hurts. I needed to forgive myself for so desperately wanting to please people and needing their approval; I would accept approval from those who gave it only if I were useful to them in some way, so I always over-gave to my own detriment.

I needed to forgive myself for not writing when I wanted; not walking or exercising when I wanted; not reading or studying for my PhD; not being me; starting things and not always finishing; for the pottery I never made; the silk screening I gave up; the judo I stopped learning; the netball I failed in; the dramatics I only did once; the choirs I never joined; the piano lessons I stopped taking; the art I failed to complete; the poetry in the bottom of the cupboard; the novels still in my head; the lunches with friends not taken; the "just for a chat" phone calls not made; the visits not enjoyed; the gym memberships wasted; the books unread; the book club never joined; the years gone; not knowing who I was when I was twenty-two; and not understanding what I felt.

I took more than an hour to let it flow. It was probably only scratching the surface. I left it open for additions as they occurred to me. Then I left it for a while. I thought of going for a walk, but instead I spent some time doing yoga.

Holding a pose to begin my yoga session, with the soles of my feet touching, hips widening, legs splayed out, resting back on a bolster, with shoulders tucked in and spine lengthened, I thought of all the things that needed forgiveness. They became two-inch wide black straps holding me down, I a Gulliver in Lilliput, but the Lilliputians had not bound me—I had. It wasn't deliberate or planned. Gradually, I asked myself to let them go. Without thinking individually of each one, as I had spent more than an hour writing them out, my mind knew what I meant. I found they turned into gossamer ribbons that gradually melted away. I felt lighter and enjoyed my yoga practice, a form of exercise I had only begun a month beforehand, beginning to relax into each pose.

I read my list six months and then twelve months later and found they held little sting, except where I wrote about forgiving myself. There I found some angst that needed further work to undertake.

After fifteen months, I searched for any physical reaction to any of the hurts. I did not have any resonance with them. Yet I would not say I have forgiven anyone. I believe I have understood and let go of the emotions that were locked in my body. There is no longer that emotional reaction of the amygdala in fight-or-flight mode charging my body with hormones to protect it. I attempted to write a list of hurts again, and all the past ones had floated away. This was not forgiveness. It was the processing of memories through a combination of journaling, EMDR therapy, meditation, yoga, and shamanic journeying.

I had been confused about forgiveness, but I am not alone.

The twelve-step Alcoholic Anonymous programme designed some seventy-five years ago requires the alcoholic make amends to the people he or she has hurt. However, the expectation is that the alcoholic forgives those who have harmed him or her without any sense that the people who have hurt this person need to make any amends at all. A young woman was told to forgive her father for not being the father she needed when he actually had emotionally abused her. She suffered PTSD, and alcohol was her socially condoned means of coping.

Before therapy, clients report incredible guilt around the harm that has occurred because of their drinking, with no granting of forgiveness toward themselves for the harm they have suffered. Some statistics claim a 17 per cent success rate with AA-type programmes. My question is, "Were the other 83 per cent of people who fail of insufficient character to forgive?" Somehow, they were not able to perform the ritual of forgiving so are to blame for keeping the hurt. This seems to me to be a re-victimisation.

Looking further, A. Orange, on the website http://www.orange-papers.org/orange-effectiveness.html, makes the claim that any success for these programmes becomes preposterous as a natural remission rate of 5 per cent seems well supported, and AA programmes don't do any better—some say even worse. One study showed the philosophy of AA was responsible for a significant increase in binge drinking, as once having taken a drink, the belief that they had no power over alcohol provided an excellent rationalisation for continuing. Rates of arrest were higher for people who attended AA than those who had no treatment. Other professional treatment showed a higher recidivism rate than the no treatment group. The worst result, though, was where there was a 3 per cent death rate among people who attended AA.

Clients at the end of a session of desensitization in EMDR therapy, with the pain attached to the memory gone, often say they no longer hate their abusers, their fathers, or their mothers, or with whomever the memory was connected. It becomes a matter of looking at the memory as in the past where it belongs and no longer feeling the fear sensations in their bodies. With the disappearance of the bodily sensations, the thoughts and beliefs about the perpetrators as needing punishment also cease to hold emotional charge.

Many years ago I met a nine-year-old who was grieving for his mother. He looked at me with the awareness of a child unencumbered by expectations. "I knew there would be someone who would make my lunch and dinner and look after me after she died. I didn't know it would hurt me so much just here." He held his hand over the centre of his tiny chest.

There are many connections that tie people to each other. They are felt in the physical body. Even when the trauma has been processed, those physical sensations that tie us through our history of experiences need to be processed as well to provide true separation. Without separation, we hold on to old hurts, old emotions. I knew this was the case for me when I noticed tension in my body following any contact or thought relating to various people. I chose a visualisation ritual to cut the ties. Sitting comfortably, I relaxed my body with slow, gentle abdominal breathing, noticing how my body felt, imagining the other person sitting opposite me. The other person's seat need not be comfortable.

I focused on my body and then an image of the other person's body, noting black smoky cords connecting different parts of our bodies. I had done this some months earlier, and the cords had been stronger and multiple but now were fewer than before and less substantial. I devoted some time to seeing where there were connecting cords, aware that even the shadow of walking beside someone left its imprint on me. The first time I had severed each cord with a sword, but tonight, in my mind, I burned them back to my flesh with a candle, allowing the flesh to turn pink and healthy in my mind. My finger was released, and then my hands and various other bits of me that had been connected. I felt a renewing energy within my pelvic area and down my legs; my hands burned warm with loving energy, and my eyes washed clear.

I continued sitting for a time within a beam of light streaming down from the cosmos through the crown of my head, filling me with healing and light. The rain outside combined with the clearing and washing away.

The repair work was done. In understanding and processing the big and little traumas of my life, I found the image of my life blossoming in a garden. Just before spring, with daffodils peeking through the frost, and sweet-smelling Daphne already blooming, the delights of raising my children, of laughter, of learning about people, in learning to cook, to counsel, to heal, to meditate, and to exercise began to push through the dirt that had covered them.

Journeying to a meadow, I meditated on the flowers in my life. There were many wildflowers and daisies, and bluebells beneath huge trees. I gratefully acknowledged the love my parents shared. The care they showed my sister and me was consistent and loving. I thanked the nurses and doctors and the scientists, like Dr. Florey, who discovered penicillin. I thanked my body for being resilient and growing stronger and healing and becoming healthy, able to sustain new life and nurture children, able to breastfeed each of them. I appreciated living at this time in history, in Australia, where there was plenty of food and sunshine and peace, where I had freedom to be educated and learn throughout my life. I picked each flower and placed it in a basket, naming it for each person who had enriched my life: my sister, my school friends, my close friends, my children and grandchildren. Each person had given me the gift of a sense of belonging, of security.

*

[19]I see myself, walking through the grass. The little bees are pollinating the flowers. The flowers grow, with long stems. I have a straw hat on, long skirt, a pinny over the top, a rush basket, reminiscent of the eighteenth century, with the long-stemmed flowers lying in the basket.

The first flowers are my parents, remembered for loving each other so much, for loving us, my sister and myself. Then there are my aunty, and my cousin. People woven through my life are like strands of a ribbon tied around—aunts, uncles, cousins, a sense of being a child in a family, of belonging.

Looking around, I see many flowers. There are many bunches of flowers. I keep one bunch beside me.

Without the hospital and medical intervention of my childhood, I would not have had this life. I would have just been a bud that fell off. So I don't bemoan it but am being grateful. I am aware of a growing awareness. People can't know what they don't know. They healed me, sent me off whole. The dentist's actions were the same. They all had to learn. They didn't know how to treat children with more compassion.

My sister, different always in health, did not know how it was for me, and not knowing is not a sin. I am grateful for the growing awareness, growing understanding, represented by opening up, closing of the flowers, for all the learning that is taking place, learning to support each other in this new urban environment. Once support was in your family, in your village. People had to learn how to do things. They have been learning for a long time. People invented things so it could be done better. The school: forgiving them, as they know not what they

[19] I described aloud what I was experiencing during the visualization journey. This is some of the edited transcript from the recording I made.

do. It is only as people become aware of how children are affected that that truth will make me (the child) free.

The sun is high and warm. Bee is in my basket, examining the flowers. There is a big bunch of flowers, bluebells under the tree. White daisies. I stand up and gather them.

One bunch, for each of my children, for Daniel not interfering, letting me love them. I feel them in my arms, at my breast, playing with their feet, their hands, caressing their heads, washing their little bodies, dressing them, holding them on my shoulder, each one of them with bunches of flowers of their own. Their father … if I hadn't had him, I wouldn't have had my children.

I am grateful for the education in an era where I didn't have to fight for it: when I didn't have to pay for it. If it had cost money, I couldn't have had it. I am grateful for the timing. It was the only time I could have done my master's degree.

I am grateful for Daniel. I had to fight against him to find my strength. I am grateful I had to seek it, as I would not have known how to be strong. I need the strength. This is the way I am meant to be, to know I am strong; I can do it. I am grateful my friends have been there, providing a sense of belonging. I am grateful my sister has again graced my life.

Perennials bloom each year. Others, like orchids, bloom less frequently, requiring the right temperature, right conditions.

Then there is a garden bed, with a wild rose, a climbing rose, that is big, covered with roses, with thorns, and a rich perfume, that fills the air with a rich, velvety fragrance. It feels like a bed of roses, as I am lying down, with roses all around me. The thought occurs that perhaps

I am dead. Someone is crying. Tears fall on my face and I disappear. My body has dissolved.

Then we walk away together.

Working It Through

If you aren't speaking the same language, it will affect your communication and your relationship. If one partner only spoke Greek and you only spoke English, you would take the time to decipher each gesture and word. You would learn each other's language. This needs to continue throughout the life of a relationship. If it hasn't, and the relationship needs repair, then looking at the languages of love is one means of beginning to rebuild.

Consider your own preferences. If someone does something for you, are you delighted or does it leave you cold?

If someone compliments you, how do you react? If flowers are brought home for you or that little something that you have been speaking about arrives unexpectedly, do you feel special or think it is a waste of money?

Do you love being hugged, or wish he would leave you alone? Can you think of nothing worse than sitting with her watching a movie when you could be working?

Then consider your partner's preferences.

How does your partner react to words of encouragement? Does she never remember what you say? Is she always too busy to go for a walk with you? Does she always complain that you never buy her flowers?

Seeking professional help to repair a relationship is a wise move. Financially, it is a lot less expensive than divorce. Emotionally, it is far easier than separation. Success may be measured in the lessening of collateral damage to other relationships. A couple may examine together the value of their relationship.

Forgiving: whom do you need to forgive? Let your mind roam.

Write down anything that comes to mind when you think of whom and what you need to forgive. Just brainstorm without trying to justify anything you note, without censoring yourself.

My list[v] included large and small hurts I perceived as inflicted by others. I included choices I had made too, actions I had done, and words I had spoken. Include things you didn't do but could have, words you didn't say but should have.

Choose a way of letting go. Meditate, or create a ritual. Breathe slowly and centre yourself. On separate pieces of paper, write each of the little hurts and the big ones. Depending upon your own preference, choose scraps of paper or special stationary. Build a fire. It doesn't have to be big. As you burn each piece of paper, let go of the hurt as you observe the smoke rise to the heavens.

Bibliography and Suggested Reading

Alexander, J. Dr. (2012). *The Hidden Psychology of Pain: The Use of Understanding to Heal Chronic Pain,* Bloomington: Balboa Press.

Bieber, J. D. (1995). *If Divorce Is the Only Way: Emotional and Practical Guide to the Essential Dos and Don'ts of Divorce and Marital Breakdown,* Ringwood, Victoria, Australia: Penguin Books.

Butler, R. N. (2011). *The Longevity Prescription: The 8 Proven Keys to a Long, Healthy Life,* Hollywood: Wiltshire Book Co.

Buzan, T. and Keene, Raymond (1996). *The Age Heresy: You Can Achieve More—Not Less—As You Get Older,* London: Ebury Press.

Chapman, G. (2004). *The Five Love Languages: The Secret to Love That Lasts,* Chicago: Northfield Publishing.

Craven, P. (2010). *Living with the Dominator,* Freedom Publishing: Great Britain.

Ellis, A. and Powers, Marcia Grad (2000). *The Secret of Overcoming Verbal Abuse:* Getting off the Emotional Roller Coaster and Regaining Control of Your Life, Hollywood: Wiltshire Book Co.

Evans, P. (2006). *The Verbally Abusive Man—Can He Change?: A Woman's Guide to Deciding Whether to Stay or Go,* Avon, MA: Adams Media.

Forward, S. (2002). *Men Who Hate Women and the Women who Love Them: When Loving Hurts and You Don't Know Why,* New York: Bantam Books.

Greer, G. (1992). *The Change: Women, Ageing, and Menopause,* London, Penguin Books.

Hislop, I. (1991). *Stress, Distress, and Illness,* Sydney: McGraw-Hill Book Company.

Houston, P., Floyd, Michael and Carnicero, Susan with Don Tennant (2012). *Spy the Lie: Former CIA Officers Teach You How to Detect Deception,* London: Icon Books.

Holy Bible, Revised Standard Version (1952). Great Britain: William Collins Sons & Co., Ltd.

Kahneman, D. (2011). *Thinking, Fast and Slow,* London; Penguin Books.

Lancer, D. (2012). *Codependency for Dummies,* Hoboken, NJ: John Wiley and Sons.

McGonigal, K. (2012). *The Willpower Instinct: How Self-Control Works, Why It Matters, and What You Can Do to Get More of It,* New York: Avery.

Miller, R. "Treatment of Behavioural Addictions Utilizing the Feeling-State Addiction Protocol: A multiple Baseline Study," *Traumatology,* 16(3) 2–10.

Millman, D. (1991). *Sacred Journey of the Peaceful Warrior,* Tiburon, CA: HJ Kramer Inc.(2000). *Way of the Peaceful Warrior: A Book that Changes Lives,* Novato, CA: New World Library.

Pagani, M., Högberg, G., Fernandez, I., & Siracusano, A. (2013). *Correlates of EMDR therapy in functional and structural neuroimaging: A critical summary of recent findings.* Journal of EMDR Practice and Research, 7(1), 29-38.

Plotkin, B. (2003). *Soulcraft: Crossing into the Mysteries of Nature and Psyche,* Novato, CA: New World Library.

Poon, A. (2009). *This Little Piggy Got Divorced: A Helpful and Humorous Handbook to Untying the Knot,* London: Spy Publishing Ltd.

Porter, E. H. (2009). *Pollyanna,* USA: Seven Treasures Publications.

Schneider, H., Dietrich, Eva S. and Venetz, Werner P. (2010). Trends and Stabilization up to 2022 in Overweight and Obesity in Switzerland, Comparison to France, UK, US, and Australia," *International Journal of Environmental Research and Public Health* (7): 460–72.

Shapiro, F. (2001). *Eye Movement Desensitization and Reprocessing: Basic Principles, Protocols, and Procedures,* 2nd Edition, New York: The Guilford Press.

Talbot, S. (2007). *The Cortisol Connection: Why Stress Makes You Fat and Ruins Your Health—and What You Can Do About It,* Alameda, CA: Hunter House Inc.

Tolle, E. (2006). *The Power of Now: A Guide to Spiritual Enlightenment,* Sydney: Hodder Australia.

Virtue, D. (2013) *The Miracles of the Archangel Gabriel,* Carlsbad, CA: Hay House Inc.

Ware, B. (2012). *The Top Five Regrets of the Dying: A Life Transformed by the Dearly Departing*, Carlsbad, CA: Hay House.

Wetzler, S. (1992). *Living With the Passive-Aggressive Man: Coping with Hidden Aggression—from the Bedroom to the Boardroom,* New York: Simon and Schuster.

Zukav, G. (2000). *Soul Stories,* Sydney: Simon and Schuster.

Websites

Australian Bureau of Statistics (2013), Divorces, retrieved from http://www.abs.gov.au/ausstats/abs@.nsf/Products/3310.0-2012-Chapter-Divorces?OpenDocument.

Artigas, L. and Jarero, Ignacio (April 2011). The Butterfly Hug Protocol retrieved from http://www.emdrtherapyvolusia.com/downloads/lynda_documents/forms_protocols_and_scripts/The_Butterfly_Hug_Protocol_April_2011.pdf.

Barger, Robert N. (2000). A Summary of Lawrence Kohlberg's Stages of Moral Development, retrieved from http://www.csudh.edu/dearhabermas/kohlberg01bk.htm, June 30, 2015.

Billings Life (Last Modified October 2012). The Billings Method of Detecting Ovulation, retrieved from http://www.thebillingsovulationmethod.org/.

Centres for Disease Control and Prevention (Injury Prevention and Control): http://www.cdc.gov/violenceprevention/acestudy/.

Cross, Joe (n.d.) http://www.rebootwithjoe.com/mean-green-juice/.

EMDR Therapy (n.d.) http://emdraa.org/.

Gangestad, S. W. and Thornhill, Randy (2008). Human Oestrus: Proc Biological Science May 7, 2008. Published online Feb 5, 2008. Retrieved from http://www.ncbi.nlm.nih.gov/pmc/articles/PMC2394562/.

What are the Possible Grounds For Annulment? (June 2015). Retrieved from http://lcdiocese.org/Annulments/grounds.htm.

National Institute on Alcohol Abuse and Alcoholism (April 1998). Alcohol and Aging retrieved from http://pubs.niaaa.nih.gov/publications/aa40.htm.

Orange, A (2014). The Effectiveness of the Twelve-Step Treatment retrieved from http://www.orange-papers.org/orange-effectiveness.html.

Osler, W (n.d.) from https://en.wikiquote.org/wiki/William_Osler.

Pope Paul VI (1968). *Encyclical Letter Humane Vitae,* 1968 Libreria Editrice Vaticana. Retrieved from http://www.vatican.va/holy_father/paul_vi/encyclicals/documents/hf_p-vi_enc_25071968_humanae-vitae_en.html

Rockstar Dinosaur Pirate Princess (2015) "Consent. It's As Simple As Tea". www.youtube.com/watch?v=oQbei5JGiT8

Rogers, S (March 3, 2011) http://scottrogerssculpture.com/rogers-gallery/women/the-othersideof17red600/.

Turner, K. (n.d.). Aging as Spiritual Awakening (Dec 2014 when last retrieved) from http://www.elderwisdom.com/ElderWisdom.com/Home_files/Aging%20as%20Spiritual%20Awakening%20-%20Link%20for%20webpage.pdf.

Felitti, V. J. MD, FACP, et al. "Relationship of Childhood Abuse and Household Dysfunction to Many of the Leading Causes of Death in Adults The Adverse Childhood Experiences (ACE) Study," *American Journal of Preventive Medicine* Volume 14, Issue 4, 245–58, Retrieved May 1998 from http://www.ajpmonline.org/article/S0749-3797(98)00017-8/abstract.

Ware, B. "The Top Five Regrets of Dying" retrieved from Susie Steiner's article in *The Guardian*, February 2012, http://www.theguardian.com/lifeandstyle/2012/feb/01/top-five-regrets-of-the-dying.

Impact of Alcohol on Aging, retrieved from http://en.wikipedia.org/wiki/Impact_of_alcohol_on_aging, December 6, 2014.

About the Author

Born to a young soldier and his bride a year after the end of the Second World War, Bryanna was in the first wave of the post-war baby boom. She was dux (top of the year) of the local girls high school. After graduating from university with a BA DipEd, majoring in mathematics and psychology, Bryanna taught for a few years in the city and the country before marrying Daniel and raising her family. She then completed further training, becoming a school guidance officer and counsellor. She worked in private and public schools for nearly twenty years before establishing a private practice at the turn of the millennium. She has an expanding number of grandchildren and a great-grandchild.

After losing weight in early 2013 as part of her recovery from emotional eating, Bryanna spent the next six months understanding how she had become so obese. She discovered the emotions that had been kept out of her conscious awareness by her obsession with her weight and dieting. This led her to recognise there were serious problems within her marriage and that no matter what she did in terms of improving communication, there was little possibility of either of them enjoying the next twenty years together.

Finally accepting that their marriage had been based on outdated assumptions that no longer applied, she concluded that continuing in the marriage was not in the best interest of either party. She applied for a divorce after more than forty years of marriage.

On the day her divorce was granted, she went to dinner with a girlfriend, who suggested champagne was obligatory. The restaurant was conducting a competition based on describing in twenty-five words or fewer the champagne moment she was celebrating. Bryanna won by writing "Tonight I am celebrating being true to myself, embracing my future beyond being a wife, mother, and grandmother." She won the contest and an all-expenses-paid trip to the Melbourne Spring Races. She deemed the universe was rewarding her.

Bryanna currently pursues a writing career and conducts workshops to assist others dealing with emotional eating, as well as seeing private clients. Bryanna has presented at conferences on EMDR, Addiction and Domestic Violence.

When Bryanna divorced Daniel, she expected to live alone. However, she is in a new nurturing relationship in which she is encouraged to value herself. Her opinions and emotions are validated. No longer on the edge of her life, she is once again forging her own way in the world.

Endnotes

i See Vincent J Felitti MD, FACP et al. "Relationship of Childhood Abuse and Household Dysfunction to Many of the Leading Causes of Death in Adults The Adverse Childhood Experiences (ACE) Study," *American Journal of Preventive Medicine*, Volume 14, Issue 4, 245–58, retrieved May 1998 from http://www.ajpmonline.org/article/S0749-3797(98)00017-8/abstract.

ii Lifeline Book Fair is an event that raises money for the Lifeline telephone helpline by selling donated books.

iii The butterfly hug describes crossing your arms across your chest, placing your middle finger under the collarbone, spreading out your other fingers, linking your thumbs to form the body of the butterfly, and then alternating lifting each hand as the wings of the butterfly. http://www.emdrtherapyvolusia.com/downloads/lynda_documents/forms_protocols_and_scripts/The_Butterfly_Hug_Protocol_April_2011.pdf.

iv The baby-boom generation is generally considered to be the children born between 1946 and 1964.

v I did not include everything on my list to protect the privacy of others.

Printed in the United States
By Bookmasters